Ranger Rick

Goes to the

National Parks!

Stacy Tornio
& Ken Keffer

muddy boots™

Published by Muddy Boots
An Imprint of The Rowman & Littlefield Publishing Group, Inc.
4501 Forbes Boulevard, Suite 200, Lanham, Maryland 20706
www.rowman.com

Unit A, Whitacre Mews, 26-34 Stannary Street, London, SE11 4AB

Distributed by NATIONAL BOOK NETWORK

Thank you for joining the National Wildlife Federation and Muddy Boots in preserving endangered animals and protecting vital wildlife habitats. The National Wildlife Federation is a voice for wildlife protection, dedicated to preserving America's outdoor traditions and inspiring generations of conservationists.

The National Wildlife Federation & Ranger Rick contributors: Mary Dalheim, John Gallagher, Ellen Lambeth, Hannah Schardt, Kathy Kranking, Michele Reyzer, Deana Duffek, Michael Morris, Kristen Ferriere, David Mizejewski, Maureen Smith.

Library of Congress Control Number: 2016910461

ISBN 978-1-63076-230-8 (paperback) 3996
ISBN 978-1-63076-231-5 (electronic)

Printed in the United States of America

Contents

See the map on the next page—The Parks are numbered so you can find them easily!

46 North Cascades
47 Olympic
45 Mount Ranier
WASHINGTON

17 Glacier
MONTANA

NORTH DAKOTA

14 Theodore Roosevelt

OREGON

18 Yellowstone
19 Grand Teton

SOUTH DAKOTA

15 Badlands
16 Wind Cave

44 Crater Lake

IDAHO

WYOMING

43 Redwood

CALIFORNIA

42 Lassen Volcanic

NEVADA

UTAH

COLORADO

NEBRASKA

41 Yosemite

Pinnacles
38
40 **39** Death Valley

Sequoia & Kings Canyon

Great Basin **35**

Arches **30**
Canyonlands **31**
Capitol Reef **32**
Zion **34** **33** Bryce Canyon

20 Rocky Mountain

22 Black Canyon of the Gunnison

23 Mesa Verde

21 Great Sand Dunes

KANSAS

37 Channel Islands

36
Joshua Tree

29 Grand Canyon

Petrified Forest **28**

ARIZONA

NEW MEXICO

OKLAHOMA

Saguaro
27

Carlsbad Caverns
24
25
Guadalupe Mountains

TEXAS

52 Gates of the Arctic
53
Kobuk Valley
ALASKA

Big Bend
26

Denali **51**
Lake Clark **54**
Katmai **55** **56**
Kenai Fjords

57 Wrangell-St. Elias

58 Glacier Bay

49 Haleakala

HAWAII
48 Hawai'i Volcanoes

50 National Park of American Samoa

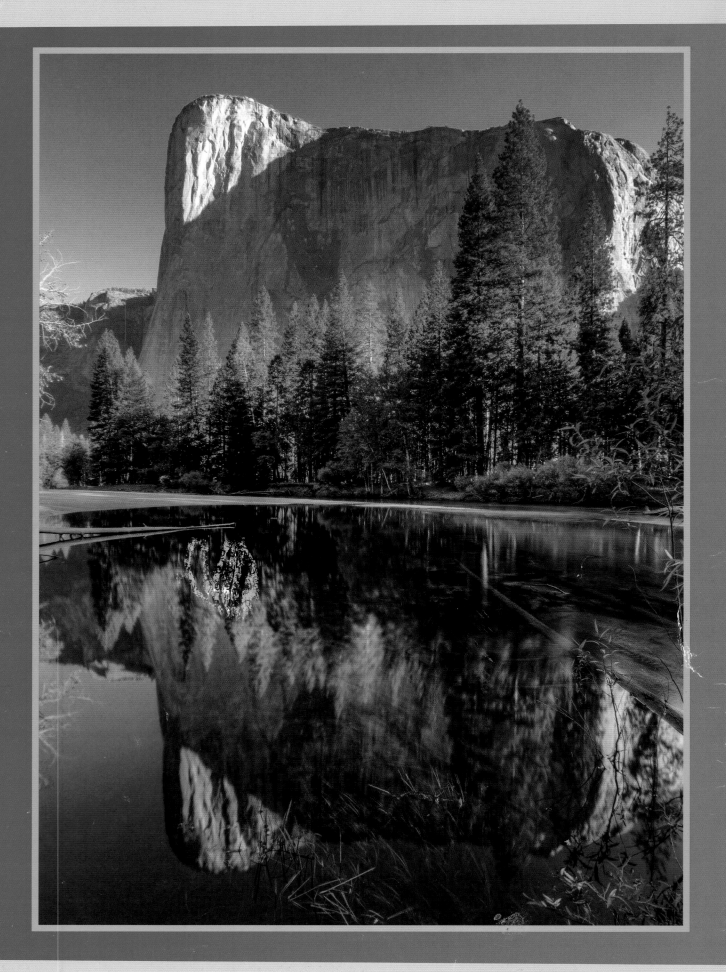

Introduction

The national park system is one of America's best treasures. Every year, millions of people travel through these wild and cherished areas to soak up the beauty, awe, and wonder of nature. While some people go to the parks for adventures like fishing, camping, backpacking, and wildlife viewing, others go for peace, solace, and to escape the hectic pace of everyday life.

Taking trips to the national parks has been part of family traditions for more than 100 years. Yellowstone was the first national park declared in 1872 by President Ulysses S. Grant. Years later, it was President Theodore Roosevelt who advanced the park system by leaps and bounds. He served as president from 1901 to 1909 and put the Antiquities Act in place in 1906. This was a big deal because it allowed the government to designate objects of historic or scientific significance for the first time. It's no wonder Roosevelt is known as the "conservation president." Much of the work he did during his presidency led to dozens of the national parks we now know today.

The National Park Service was officially created in 1916. President Woodrow Wilson signed the act to create this new federal bureau. It was an important and historical moment, and from then on, all the national parks, monuments, and land would officially be protected. Plus, all future parks would be in good hands, too.

All great things should be celebrated, and the birthday of the National Park Service is no different. The year 2016 marks a significant milestone—100 years of this important

program and a reminder of why it's so important to protect these lands.

The next time you go a national park, think about all the people that worked to make it possible. Without the National Park Service or laws to protect these lands, these areas could have been turned into anything—cities, rows of houses, or even miles and miles of highways.

Even more important is to share your love of the national parks with others. These parks represent some of the only wild and untouched land left in the United States. It's up to us to respect them, protect them, and visit them so they stay beautiful and special for another 100, 200, and 500 years.

Woody Guthrie was a singer-songwriter popular in the 1930s and 1940s, and he wrote one of the most famous songs that people associate with the national parks. The lyrics are still important and ring true today.

This land is your land,
This land is my land,
From California, to the New York Island
From the redwood forest, to the Gulf Stream waters
This land was made for you and me.

How to Use This Book

This book is made to go wherever you go. Take it to school with you to share cool national parks facts with your teachers and friends. Throw it in your vacation bag to read up on the parks you want to visit next. And bring it along on trips to the national parks to help you decide what to see and do.

Above all, this book should serve as inspiration. Think of it as a jumping off point. Yes, it highlights some of the coolest spots and treasures at each park, but don't stop there. Do those things on the list, but then go and find your own adventures, too.

Every single national park in the United States is highlighted in this book. The most popular and visited parks have expanded entries with more things to learn, look for, and do. But every single entry will give you a feel for each park, and you'll discover places you want to go that you never even knew about. Look for these four things highlighted for each park.

About the Park: It gives a quick overview and some basic facts.

Ranger Rick's Top Nature Picks: Ranger Rick's top plants and animals to look for.

Ranger Rick's Top Things to Do: Ranger Rick's top choices for activities in each park.

Ranger Rick's Amazing Facts: Ranger Rick's "wow" facts about each park.

You should always make your first stop the Visitor Center. Think of park rangers as your own personal travel agent for the national parks. They'll be able to tell you the most up-to-date information, but they'll also give you hints to make your trip the most enjoyable experience possible. Perhaps there is a really cool wildlife sighting nearby. Or maybe they are offering up a neat interpretive program later that day. With the help of a park ranger, you can even become a Junior Ranger!

About the Park
Location: Coastal Maine
Size: 47,390 acres
Famous for: First national park east of the Mississippi River
Established: 1919

Acadia National Park

From splashing seas to high granite peaks, Acadia National Park is a diverse and rugged landscape. Equally as vital to the park is its cultural history, which is ever present from the iconic carriage roads to the Bass Harbor Head Lighthouse. Much of what is now Acadia National Park was donated by wealthy families, including the Rockefellers, Fords, and Vanderbilts who had taken up residence in the area but were concerned about development threatening the natural wonders of the region.

What to Watch For

moose
white-tailed deer
peregrine falcon
blueberry

white-tailed deer

peregrine falcon chick

blueberry

Ranger Rick's TOP 5 Things to Do in ACADIA National Park

1 Take in the view from the top of Mount Cadillac. At 1,530 feet tall, it's the highest point along the Atlantic Coast.

2 Take a carriage ride, or bike along the historic broken stone roads. Look closely at the 17 stone-faced bridges of the area. Each one is unique.

3 Go tidepooling at low tide. Bar Island Sand Bar, Sand Beach, Ship Harbor, and Wonderland are some of the best areas.

4 Become an EarthCacher. EarthCaching is part GPS navigating and part scavenger hunt. The Acadia EarthCache Program is a fun way to see the park and to learn about the geologic history of the area.

5 Explore the Schoodic Peninsula by foot, bike, or car.

Ranger Rick's AMAZING FACTS About ACADIA National Park

- During parts of the year, it is the first spot in the United States to see the sunrise.

- The Wild Gardens of Acadia highlight the natural habitats found throughout Mount Desert Island.

- Isle au Haut translates to "high island." This unit of Acadia is a great place to hike and offers up a remote camping experience. You'll have to take a boat ride to get here though.

- Acadia National Park has recorded 338 species of birds.

- Whale watching is a popular pastime around Acadia. Also keep a look out for harbor seals bobbing in the ocean water.

moose

About the Park

Location: Northeast Ohio
Size: 32,861 acres
Established: 2000
Famous for: Preserving cultural and natural resources along the Cuyahoga River

Cuyahoga Valley National Park

Nearly 25 miles of the Cuyahoga River are protected within this park tucked between Cleveland and Akron, Ohio. Cuyahoga Valley is a great place for year-round outdoor fun. Visit the park for hiking and biking in the summer or cross country skiing in the winter.

What to Watch For

raccoon
great blue heron
oak-hickory forests
painted turtle

great blue heron

raccoon

painted turtle

Ranger Rick's
Top Thing to Do
in CUYAHOGA VALLEY
National Park

Hope on board the Cuyahoga Valley Scenic Railroad. Trains have had a history in the Cuyahoga Valley since the 1880s. The CVSR used to haul coal, but now people ride it through the park from the Rockside Station in the north to the Akron Northside Station in the south. You can even bring a bike on board and peddle your way back to where you started.

Ranger Rick's
TOP FACT About
CUYAHOGA VALLEY
National Park

The historic Ohio & Erie Canal was finished in 1832. The Towpath Trail in the park follows this path for nearly 20 miles. The 11 trailheads lead visitors to historic structures and through natural areas. When on the trail, give questing a try. Questing is like geocaching without a GPS.

Shenandoah National Park

Just a 75-mile drive from the United States capital, Washington, DC, Shenandoah National Park is a showcase along the crest of the Blue Ridge Mountains. Skyline Drive is the 105-mile scenic highway through the park, but don't just ride around in the car—get out and explore.

What to Watch For

bobcat
Virginia opossum
white-tailed deer
tulip poplar
scarlet tanager

scarlet tanager

About the Park

Location: Northern Virginia
Size: 199,045 acres
Established: 1926
Famous for: Scenic Blue Ridge Mountains of Virginia

white-tailed deer

Virginia opossum

Ranger Rick's **Top Thing to Do** in SHENANDOAH National Park

Skyline Drive has 75 overlook pullouts, but Shenandoah, like all national parks, should be explored beyond the pavement. There are over 500 miles of trails, including nearly 100 miles of the Appalachian Trail (which runs from Georgia to Maine).

Ranger Rick's **TOP FACT** About SHENANDOAH National Park

Shenandoah is home to many cascades and waterfalls, especially in the spring and after it rains. To get to the most spectacular waterfalls, like Rose River, South River, and Jones Run Falls, will require a bit of a hike. The views will be totally worth it!

bobcat

tulip poplar

About the Park

Location: Along the North Carolina and Tennessee borders
Size: 521,490 acres
Established: 1934
Famous for: Most visited national park

black bear

Great Smoky Mountains National Park

Not only is Great Smoky Mountains the most visited national park, it is also one of the most diverse parks for both plant and animal life. The forested ridges of Great Smoky Mountains are a highlight of the southern Appalachian region. From bald mountains to cascading streams, Great Smoky Mountains is a natural paradise.

What to Watch For

black bear
elk
cerulean warbler
ginseng
black-chinned red salamander

cerulean warbler

black-chinned red salamander

elk

Ranger Rick's TOP 5 Things to Do in GREAT SMOKY MOUNTAINS National Park

1 Hike to a waterfall. Indian Creek Falls is an easy 1.6-mile round-trip hike and offers a bonus waterfall, Tom Branch Falls, along the way. Other more moderate hikes include trips to see Rainbow, Laurel, and Hen Wallow Falls.

2 Cades Cove Loop Road is the most popular bike-riding place in Great Smoky Mountains, but you might also want to bike along Greenbrier, Lakeview Drive, Cataloochee, or Tremont Road.

3 Great Smoky Mountains is one of the East's best spots for trout fishing. Grab a fishing pole (and a license) and try your hand at fishing.

4 Look for elk in the Smokies. This species was re-introduced to the national park in 2001. The southeastern region of the park, in the Cataloochee area, is the best spot for viewing these majestic mammals.

5 Fall can be a great time to visit the Smokies. Parts of the park are in peak fall foliage from early October to early November.

Ranger Rick's AMAZING FACTS About GREAT SMOKY MOUNTAINS National Park

- Clingmans Dome is the highest peak in the Smokies and the third highest east of the Mississippi River. It has an elevation of 6,643 feet.

- Ramsey Cascades is the tallest waterfall in the park, and it is also home to many of the salamanders that the Smokies are famous for.

- Cable Mill and Mingus Mill are two water-powered grist mills that operate in the park from mid-March to mid-November.

- The Blue Ridge Parkway connects Great Smoky Mountains to Shenandoah National Park, 469 scenic highway miles away.

APPALACHIAN TRAIL
Sweat Heifer Creek Trail   1.7
Boulevard Trail   2.7
Katahdin Maine   1972.0

Hot Springs National Park

Hot Springs National Park is like no other park in the entire system. It highlights natural springs and historic bathhouses, collectively nicknamed "The American Spa." The park is tucked in the Ouachita Mountains and includes 26 miles of nature trails.

About the Park

Location: Hot Springs, Arkansas
Size: 5,550 acres
Established: 1921
Famous for: Preserving historic hot springs and bathhouses

raccoon

green treefrog

red-bellied woodpecker

What to Watch For

raccoon

green treefrog

Ouachita red-backed salamander

pine-oak-hickory forest

red-bellied woodpecker

Ranger Rick's Top Thing to Do in HOT SPRINGS National Park

Stroll along Bathhouse Row. Be sure to visit the historic Fordyce Bathhouse, where you'll be able to see, touch, and even taste the water of the hot springs. You'll get a glimpse back in time to the early 1900s as you tour the most extravagant of bathhouses.

Ranger Rick's TOP FACT About HOT SPRINGS National Park

Many baseball teams held spring training in Hot Springs, Arkansas, from the 1880s to the 1940s. Players would soak in the hot springs water after their games.

About the Park

Location: Southcentral Kentucky
Size: 52,830 acres
Established: 1941
Famous for: Most extensive cave system in the world

Mammoth Cave National Park

Don't be fooled by the name here because there is more to Mammoth Cave than the cave itself. The park offers the chance to hike, canoe, horseback ride, picnic, camp, and more. But be sure to take a tour of the cave, too!

What to Watch For

**little brown bat
northern cavefish
cave crayfish
rough pigtoe mussel
trout lily**

trout Lily

little brown bat

Ranger Rick's
Top Thing to Do
in MAMMOTH CAVE
National Park

Make it your mission to find some troglodytes.
(This is just a word for "cave-dwelling species.")
You can find northern cavefish, cave crayfish,
Kentucky cave shrimp, and cave snails.

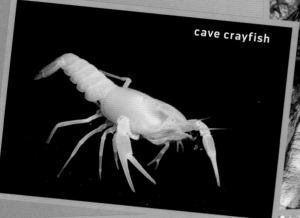

cave crayfish

Ranger Rick's **TOP FACT**
About MAMMOTH CAVE
National Park

The troglodytes aren't the only rare
species found in Mammoth Cave
National Park. A section of the Green
River that flows through the park
(left) hosts more freshwater mussel
species—including the funny-named
rough pigtoe, the sheepnose, and the
ring pink—than anywhere else.

About the Park
Location: Central South Carolina
Size: 26,546 acres
Established: 2003
Famous for: Largest remaining area of old-growth bottomland hardwood forest

Congaree National Park

One of the newest parks, Congaree National Park showcases the amazing biodiversity of the Southeast. It is sometimes referred to as the "Redwoods of the East" because of the huge trees that grow in the area.

barred owl

green anole

What to Watch For

barred owl
green anole
bald cypress
loblolly pine
spanish moss

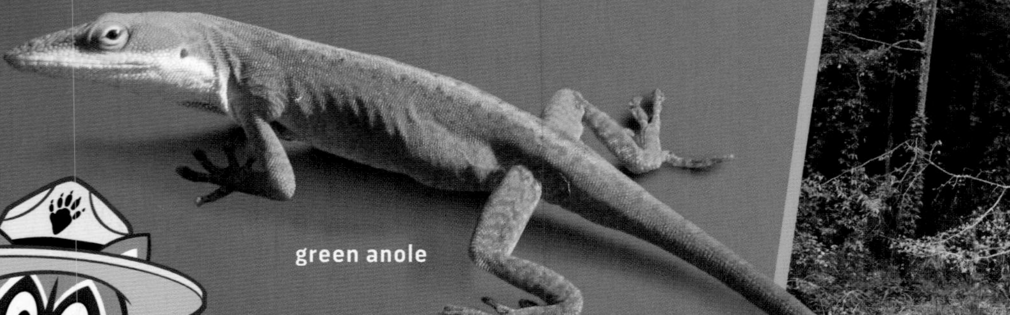

spanish moss

Ranger Rick's Top Thing to Do
in CONGAREE National Park

Hiking on trails is a great way to explore Congaree National Park. A 2-mile long boardwalk lets you experience Cedar Creek without getting your feet wet. The Cedar Creek Canoe Trail is 15 miles long and winds its way through the Congaree Wilderness. Hopefully your feet will stay dry on your canoe adventure, too, otherwise you flipped your boat. If you're really up for adventure, consider the 50-mile Congaree River Blue Trail. Start in Columbia and paddle downstream to Congaree.

Ranger Rick's
TOP FACT
About CONGAREE National Park

Congaree is home to over a dozen Champion Trees, the largest tree known for each species. The tallest Loblolly Pine is 167 feet, or about the height of a 16 story tall building. Other Champion Trees include Sweetgum (157 feet), American Elm (135 feet) and Common Persimmon (127 feet).

bald cypress

About the Park
Location: Southern Florida
Size: 1.5 milion acres
Established: 1934
Famous for: The largest subtropical wilderness in the United States

Everglades National Park

Everglades National Park, a World Heritage Site, is a huge expanse of wetland habitats as freshwater drains from Lake Okeechobee to the Florida Bay. Fields of sawgrass are dotted with slightly elevated hammocks of trees.

What to Watch For

Florida panther
American alligator
anhinga
manatee
sawgrass

manatee

Florida panther

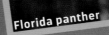
American alligator

anhinga

sawgrass

Ranger Rick's
Top Thing to Do
in EVERGLADES
National Park

From the 65-foot-tall observation tower at Shark Valley to the 99-mile Wilderness Waterway canoe trail, there are numerous ways to see Everglades National Park. For a hands-on, (actually it's more of a feet-on) learning experience, join an Everglades Park Ranger for some Slough Slogging. These guided walks wade off-trail through the River of Grass that is the Everglades.

Ranger Rick's **TOP FACT** About
EVERGLADES National Park

From the royal palm to the Florida panther, the Everglades host unique species, many of which are found nowhere else in the United States. There are over 700 species of plants found in the Everglades. Nearly 350 species of birds have been reported. Everglades are also home to numerous species of animals that are not native to the region, including Burmese pythons. These nonnative species all compete with the native species of the region.

About the Park

Location: South Florida
Size: 172,924 acres
Established: 1980
Famous for: Islands, coral reefs, and the scenic waters off the coast of Miami

Biscayne National Park

Biscayne National Park is a stark contrast to downtown Miami, despite being just offshore. Since 95% of the park is water, you'll need to take a boat ride to really explore. Snorkeling is another option for experiencing Biscayne at its finest.

hawksbill sea turtle

manatee

What to Watch For

manatee
American crocodile
hawksbill sea turtle
mangrove
sargent's palm

American crocodile

Ranger Rick's **Top Thing to Do** in BISCAYNE National Park

Elliott Key, the largest island of Biscayne National Park, is home to the only hiking trail within this mostly aquatic park. Boca Chita is home to Biscayne's iconic lighthouse.

Ranger Rick's **TOP FACT** About BISCAYNE National Park

Biscayne National Park was once dominated by farms of pineapples and key limes. Now it is a recreation paradise for boaters, snorkelers, campers, and for wildlife enthusiasts.

mangrove

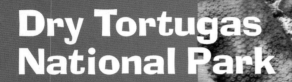

Dry Tortugas National Park

Dry Tortugas is a remote national park that has spectacular nature. You can only get to Dry Tortugas by boat or seaplane. It is made up of seven islands and the surrounding marine environments. Loggerhead Key is the largest island.

About the Park

Location: 70 miles west of Key West, Florida
Size: 64,701 acres
Established: 1992
Famous for: Beautiful and undisturbed coral reefs

corals

magnificent frigatebird

What to Watch For

corals
magnificent frigatebird
sooty tern
loggerhead sea turtle
green sea turtle

loggerhead hatchlings

Ranger Rick's **Top Thing to Do** in DRY TORTUGAS National Park

Visitors to Garden Key, the second largest island of Dry Tortugas, can't avoid Fort Jefferson when they arrive. Take a guided tour to learn about the historical significance of this masonry fort. It helped protected the waters from enemy ships during the 1800s.

Ranger Rick's **TOP FACT** About DRY TORTUGAS National Park

The coral environment of Dry Tortugas is a safe-haven for nesting loggerhead and green sea turtles. It is the also the only place in the United States where magnificent frigatebirds and sooty terns nest.

green sea turtle

Virgin Islands National Park

On the island of St. John, Virgin Islands National Park is split between terrestrial areas (on land) and aquatic habitats (under the water). Virgin Islands National Park is richly beautiful from lush landscapes and barren desert to underwater coral reefs of stunning diversity.

greater bulldog bat

What to Watch For

corals
greater bulldog bat
dwarf gecko
green sea turtle
seagrass

seagrass

corals

Ranger Rick's Top Thing to Do in VIRGIN ISLANDS National Park

Virgin Islands National Park (and the Virgin Islands Coral Reef National Monument) is a snorkeler and diver's paradise. There are over 50 different kinds of coral here. The structure of coral comes from seawater calcium. Colonies of coral grow together to form coral reefs. Trunk Bay even has an Underwater Trail for snorkeling.

sugar mill

Ranger Rick's TOP FACT About VIRGIN ISLANDS National Park

During the 1700s and early 1800s, sugar was king on the island of St. John. Much evidence of large scale sugar factories is still present. Peace Hill Windmill, Trunk Bay Sugar Factory, Annaberg Plantation, Reef Bay Factory, and many other sites provide a glimpse into the past at Virgin Islands National Park.

About the Park
Location: Lake Superior, Michigan
Size: 571,790 acres
Established: 1940
Famous for: Largest island in the largest freshwater lake in the world, Lake Superior.

Isle Royale National Park

You'll have to make a summertime visit—the park is closed in winter. But for those willing to make the trip, Isle Royale provides a wilderness setting that can't be beat. This national park isn't on the way to anywhere. It is remotely located on an island in Lake Superior, far off the coast of Michigan's Upper Peninsula.

common loon

What to Watch For

moose
gray wolf
common loon
elegant lichen
balsam fir

gray wolf

Ranger Rick's Top Thing to Do in ISLE ROYALE National Park

Most visitors arrive on Isle Royale by taking one of the ferry boats. Access to the park is so limited that making a day trip hardly seems worth it. Instead, plan on camping out for a night or two. Out of all of the national parks, Isle Royale has the the highest rates of backcountry camping per acre, but there is plenty of wild in the park for all visitors.

wolf tracks

moose

Ranger Rick's TOP FACT About ISLE ROYALE National Park

Isle Royale only has around 20 species of mammals (including six different bats), while mainland areas nearby have 40 species. Some critters get to these isolated islands by swimming or by walking across frozen Lake Superior. The island has provided researchers a unique opportunity to study predator-prey interactions with wolves and moose for over 50 years.

About the Park

Location: Northern Minnesota
Size: 218,200 acres
Established: 1971
Famous for: Gorgeous waters throughout the park, which kayakers, canoeists, and others love

Voyageurs National Park

The area of Voyageurs National Park is a landscape of forests and water. The region was initially explored by French-Canadian fur traders and has changed little since then.

river otters

beaver

What to Watch For

gray wolf
river otter
common loon
beaver
black spruce

Ranger Rick's Top Thing to Do in VOYAGEURS National Park

Paddling is the best way to see Voyageurs National Park. Even if you don't have your own boat, you can experience the water on the North Canoe Voyage which departs from the Rainy Lake Visitor Center. These tours are in 26-foot North Canoes.

Ranger Rick's TOP FACT About VOYAGEURS National Park

A portage is the term for carrying your canoe over land. The 68 mile Kabetogama Peninsula Loop Canoe Paddle requires two portages: one at Kettle Falls Dam and the other at Gold Portage.

Theodore Roosevelt National Park

Teddy Roosevelt's time in North Dakota shaped the conservation ethic he is known for. As president, he signed the 1906 American Antiquities Act for protecting wildlife and public lands. President Roosevelt protected 230 million acres of public lands as national forests, bird or game preserves, and national parks and monuments. Fittingly, his ranch properties are now protected as Theodore Roosevelt National Park.

About the Park
Location: Western North Dakota
Size: 70,447 acres
Established: 1978
Famous for: Rugged badlands and the former ranch properties of Teddy Roosevelt

western meadowlark

What to Watch For

bison
black-footed ferret
prairie rattlesnake
black-tailed prairie dog
western meadowlark

black-footed ferret

prairie rattlesnake

black-tailed prairie dog

Ranger Rick's
Top Thing to Do
in THEODORE ROOSEVELT
National Park

Now under the management of Theodore Roosevelt National Park, the Maltese Cross Cabin (at the South Unit Visitor Center) and the Elkhorn Ranch property (midway between the North and South Units of the national park) provided Teddy Roosevelt a place to heal after his mother and wife both died in February 1884. Definitely make plans to see it. The park continues to maintain a small herd of longhorn cattle to celebrate the ranching and cattle drive heritage of the region.

bison

pronghorn

Ranger Rick's TOP FACT About
THEODORE ROOSEVELT National Park

This national park is one of the best places to view the famous North Dakota Badlands, which is one of the few areas of wilderness left in the Northern Great Plains area. Jump on a section of the 36-mile scenic loop and you'll experience several spectacular views, including some of the local prairie dog towns.

About the Park
Location: Western South Dakota
Size: 242,756 acres
Established: 1978
Famous for: Rugged badlands and prairie landscapes

Badlands National Park

Wind and water erosion sculpt out impressive badlands within the vast grasslands of South Dakota. Badlands National Park is a haven for wildlife, and a popular place for hiking, camping, and stargazing.

What to Watch For

bighorn sheep
bison
swift fox
black-footed ferret
burrowing owl

bighorn sheep

bison

Ranger Rick's
Top Thing to Do
in BADLANDS National Park

Visit the restored Maltese Cross Cabin to see Teddy Roosevelt's writing desk and trunk. You might also spot a herd of longhorn cattle grazing the property. The park maintains the small herd of longhorns to celebrate the ranching and cattle drive heritage of the region.

finding fossils

swift fox

Ranger Rick's
TOP FACT
About BADLANDS National Park

Badlands National Park showcases the rugged badlands and prairie streams of western North Dakota's Northern Great Plains landscape. Herds of bison and pronghorn still roam the hills here. Black-footed ferrets and swift foxes are nocturnal, so they're rarely seen. Instead, keep your eyes peeled for roaming bison and bighorn sheep.

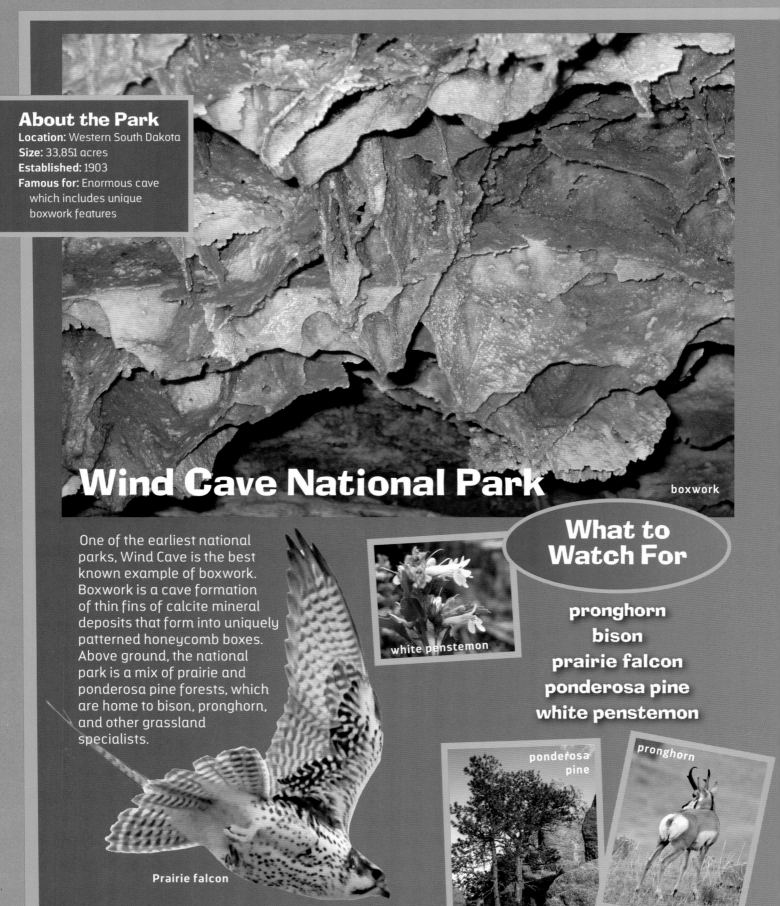

Wind Cave National Park

boxwork

One of the earliest national parks, Wind Cave is the best known example of boxwork. Boxwork is a cave formation of thin fins of calcite mineral deposits that form into uniquely patterned honeycomb boxes. Above ground, the national park is a mix of prairie and ponderosa pine forests, which are home to bison, pronghorn, and other grassland specialists.

white penstemon

Prairie falcon

What to Watch For

pronghorn
bison
prairie falcon
ponderosa pine
white penstemon

ponderosa pine

pronghorn

Ranger Rick's
Top Thing to Do
in WIND CAVE
National Park

Wind Cave National Park offers cave tours throughout the year. Shorter tours like the Natural Entrance and Fairgrounds Tours give visitors a glimpse of the stunning features and history of the cave. Longer tours like the Candlelight Tour give visitors a deeper look at the depths of Wind Cave.

Ranger Rick's TOP FACT
About WIND CAVE National Park

Wind Cave is named after the wind, but not just because the plains are a windy place. The differences in barometric pressures outside of and within the cave create its own wind, which has been clocked at over 70 miles per hour.

About the Park
Location: Northwest Montana
Size: 1,013,572 acres
Established: 1910
Famous for: Glaciers, lakes, mountainous landscapes, and wildlife

Glacier National Park

On the border of Montana, USA, and Alberta, Canada, Glacier National Park is a part of the larger Waterton-Glacier International Peace Park. Named for the numerous high elevation glaciers, the national park has some of the most stunning landscapes in the world.

What to Watch For

mountain goat
grizzly bear
harlequin duck
beargrass
golden-mantled ground squirrel

bighorn sheep

grizzly bear

golden-mantled ground squirrel

harlequin duck

Ranger Rick's
Top Thing to Do
in GLACIER National Park

The 50 mile Going–to-the-Sun Road was dedicated in 1933. During the brief summer, this is the main route through the park. Portions of the road remain open all year, but Logan Pass is closed seasonally due to excessive snows. Logan Pass marks the divide along the road, and from here you can scan the mountains for rock climbers (both human and animal).

historic red jammer bus

beargrass

mountain goat

Ranger Rick's TOP FACT
About GLACIER National Park

Climbers aren't the only ones going up the peaks in Glacier National Park. It is one of the best spots to see shaggy white mountain goats and brown bighorn sheep. Both billy (male) and nanny (female) mountain goats have black horns that curve back slightly. Bighorn sheep ewes (females) have brown horns that look similar to mountain goats, but the rams (males) have massive horns that can nearly curl around into a full circle.

old faithful

About the Park

Location: Northwest Wyoming, and adjacent Montana & Idaho

Size: 2,219,791 acres

Established: 1872

Famous for: The first national park

Yellowstone National Park

Yellowstone National Park protects the largest concentration of geysers and geothermal features in the world. It is also a wildlife hotspot with many documented species, including 67 mammals, 330 birds, 16 fish, and 11 reptiles and amphibians.

What to Watch For

**grizzly bear
elk
red squirrel
Yellowstone cutthroat trout
gray wolf**

grizzly bear

Grand Canyon of the Yellowstone

Yellowstone cutthroat trout

red squirrel

river rafting

Ranger Rick's TOP 5 Things to Do in YELLOWSTONE National Park

1 Old Faithful is the star of the geothermal show in Yellowstone, but there are other awesome geysers, mud pots, and hot springs to check out—including Morning Glory Pool, Grand Prismatic Spring, and Fountain Paint Pot.

2 Did you know Yellowstone has a Grand Canyon of its very own? The Grand Canyon of the Yellowstone is about 20 miles long. Upper Falls are 109 feet tall, while Lower Falls plunge 308 feet downward. Artist Point is one of the must-see areas in Yellowstone for incredible views of the canyon.

3 You can't fish at Fishing Bridge, but much of Yellowstone is open for world-class trout fishing. Give fly-fishing a try, and remember that Yellowstone National Park rules require catch-and-release fishing for native cutthroat trout.

4 Make sure you take a hike when you visit Yellowstone. From short day hikes to multi-day backcountry adventures, Yellowstone has over 900 miles of trail.

5 Whether traveling by snowcoach or snowmobile, the winter experience in Yellowstone is a spectacular landscape of snow and beauty. Take a ski or a snowshoe hike to gain a full appreciation of winter in Yellowstone.

nanny mountain goat with her kid

fresh snow on Soda Butte Creek

bison

Grand Prismatic Spring

Ranger Rick's AMAZING FACTS About YELLOWSTONE National Park

- The best times for seeing wildlife are early mornings and in the evenings. Some of the best locations to see the iconic critters of Yellowstone include Hayden, Pelican, and Lamar Valleys.

- You can't fish at Fishing Bridge, but much of Yellowstone is open for world-class trout fishing. Unfortunately, native cutthroat trout populations (as well as other species that depend on them for survival) have been affected by the release of Lake Trout into Yellowstone Lake.

- Fire has always played a role in shaping the Yellowstone landscape. Lodgepole pines have cones that only release their seeds after being burned. Species such as fireweed and three-toed woodpeckers quickly establish themselves in areas following fires.

- There are over 300 geysers in Yellowstone. Steamboat Geyser is the world's tallest, but it rarely erupts.

- Fringed gentian is the official flower of Yellowstone National Park.

gray wolf

About the Park
Location: Northwest Wyoming
Size: 309,995 acres
Established: 1929
Famous for: Stunning landscape and abundant wildlife

Grand Teton National Park

Connected to Yellowstone National Park by the John D. Rockefeller Memorial Parkway, Grand Teton National Park is a postcard-worthy landscape of rugged mountains rising above the valley floor and the Snake River. The park is also a noted wildlife viewing area, especially for moose, bison, coyotes, river otters, and numerous birds.

What to Watch For

bison
river otter
masked shrew
trumpeter swan
willows

masked shrew

river otter

willows

trumpeter swan

Ranger Rick's Top Thing to Do in GRAND TETON National Park

There isn't a bad view anywhere in Grand Teton National Park. An especially epic perspective is from Jenny Lake. You can take a short ferryboat ride across Jenny Lake to the base of the mountains. But you'll have a better chance of spotting a black bear and other wildlife if you hike the trail! The Snake River also provides excellent wildlife viewing opportunities.

elk

bison herd

Ranger Rick's TOP FACT About GRAND TETON National Park

The Tetons are composed of some of the oldest rocks in North America, and yet they are one of the youngest mountain ranges in the world. In fact, they are still growing at a rate of about half an inch per year. To get a more panoramic view of the mountains, try the Oxbow Bend, Two Ocean Lake Road, or Antelope Flats.

About the Park
Location: Northcentral Colorado
Size: 265,828 acres
Established: 1915
Famous for: Spectacular mountain environments

Rocky Mountain National Park

The mighty Colorado River starts out as a mere trickle in Rocky Mountain National Park. Situated high in the central Rockies, along the Continental Divide, the park is a recreation paradise all year long. A fall drive is especially impressive as the aspen leaves shimmer gold and provide the backdrop for bugling elk.

What to Watch For

elk
beaver
American dipper
boreal toad
aspen

aspen

elk

American dipper

beaver

Ranger Rick's
Top Thing to Do
in ROCKY MOUNTAIN National Park

Trail Ridge Road, the highest road in any national park, will takes travelers over 12,000 feet in elevation. From here there are numerous scenic vistas and access to many of the 300 miles of trails that crisscross Rocky Mountain National Park.

Trail Ridge Road

bighorn sheep

Ranger Rick's TOP FACT
About ROCKY MOUNTAIN National Park

Longs Peak has an elevation of 14,259 feet, and much of Rocky Mountain National Park is above the timber line. Alpine plants are adapted to survive these harsh conditions, and the trees are stunted and twisted by the winds (called krummholz).

Great Sand Dunes National Park

When you think of sand dunes, you might imagine the ocean coast, but the tallest dunes in North America are found in Colorado at Great Sand Dunes National Park. The park is more than just sand, though. It includes diverse ecosystems from grasslands, to forests, to alpine tundra. Many rare dune plants and cool critters thrive here.

What to Watch For

pronghorn
Ord's kangaroo rat
Rio Grande cutthroat trout
great sand dunes tiger beetle
sandhill cranes

About the Park

Location: Southcentral Colorado
Size: 42,984 acres
Established: 2004
Famous for: Tallest sand dunes in North America

pronghorn

Great Sand Dunes tiger beetle

Ranger Rick's Top Thing to Do in GREAT SAND DUNES National Park

Here is something you can't do in many places: sand sledding. Sand sleds are specially designed to glide on the sand. You might find using a little wax will help. Sand sledding is lots of fun. Just remember to be safe and to be careful not to sled over the top of any delicate dune plants.

sandhill cranes

Ranger Rick's TOP FACT About GREAT SAND DUNES National Park

Great Sand Dunes National Park even has a beach of its own, at least for a few months. Medano Creek is a seasonal stream that begins in the melting snowfields of the nearby mountains.

About the Park
Location: Western Colorado
Size: 32,950 acres
Established: 1999
Famous for: Incredibly rugged and deep canyon along the Gunnison River

Black Canyon of the Gunnison National Park

Over the course of a couple of million years, the Gunnison River carved out the 2,000-foot deep Black Canyon. The Black Canyon of the Gunnison National Park covers about 14 miles. Other stretches of the 53-mile canyon are protected in the Gunnison Gorge National Conservation Area and the Curecanti National Recreation Area.

What to Watch For

mule deer
rock squirrel
peregrine falcon
striped whipsnake
pinyon/juniper forests

peregrine falcon

striped whipsnake

mule deer

Ranger Rick's
Top Thing to Do
in BLACK CANYON OF THE GUNNISON National Park

Hikers can get a good feel for the scale of the canyon by hiking the Rim Rock Nature Trail on the South Rim of the canyon or the Chasm View Nature Trail on the North Rim.

Ranger Rick's
TOP FACT About BLACK CANYON OF THE GUNNISON National Park

The steep and narrow Black Canyon of the Gunnison is a destination for expert rock climbers. It is also popular with expert kayakers.

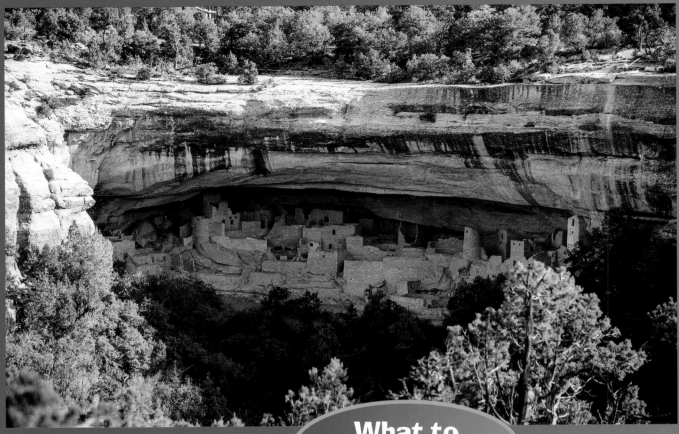

Mesa Verde National Park

Mesa Verde National Park covers a portion of the Ancestral Pueblo peoples' homeland from AD 600 to 1300. The site protects over 6,000 archeological sites, most notably over 600 cliff dwellings as well as pithouses, pueblos, masonry towers, and farming structures.

coyote

What to Watch For

mule deer
porcupine
juniper titmouse
Cliff Palace milkvetch
coyote

juniper titmouse

mule deer

porcupine

About the Park
Location: Southwest Colorado
Size: 52,122 acres
Established: 1906
Famous for: Protecting over 600 cliff dwellings of the Ancestral Pueblo people

Ranger Rick's
Top Thing to Do
in MESA VERDE National Park

A few dwellings, such as Spruce Tree House, are open to self-guided tours for much of the year. To really appreciate and understand Mesa Verde National Park, take a ranger-guided tour of the cliff dwellings. The 150-room Cliff Palace is the largest cliff dwelling in North America. Balcony House is another popular ranger-guided option, although it is closed during the winter months.

Ranger Rick's **TOP FACT** About
MESA VERDE National Park

The Ancestral Puebloans spent 600 years living atop the mesa before building their dwellings beneath the overhanging cliffs around the year 1200. They lived here for less than 100 years before moving southward to present day New Mexico and Arizona.

Carlsbad Caverns National Park

Carlsbad Caverns National Park includes a vast network of caves, as well as a vast region of the Chihuahuan Desert along the Guadalupe Mountains. The Guadalupes and the caverns formed from a reef in an ancient sea. The Big Room, within the park's namesake cave, is the largest single cave chamber in North America.

About the Park

Location: Southeastern New Mexico
Size: 46,766 acres
Established: 1930
Famous for: More than 119 limestone caves in the park

ringtail

What to Watch For

Brazilian free-tailed bats
ringtail
cave swallow
cave cricket
Mormon tea

cave cricket

Mormon tea

Ranger Rick's **Top Thing to Do** in CARLSBAD CAVERNS National Park

While there are more than 119 caves in Carlsbad Caverns National Park, only a few are open for public viewing. Ranger-led programs will take visitors to places otherwise off-limits. Carlsbad Cavern itself can be explored via two self-guided trails. The Big Room Trail is the easier of the two. Natural Entrance Trail has an extremely steep slope as you descend 750 feet into the cavern. The cave is always about 56 degrees Fahrenheit.

Ranger Rick's **TOP FACT** About CARLSBAD CAVERNS National Park

There are 17 species of bats in the park, but the Brazilian free-tailed bats of Carlsbad Cavern steal the show. Bat flight programs are offered in the evenings (except in the winter when the bats migrate). Visitors watch as hundreds of thousands of Brazilian free-tailed bats head out into the darkness in search of bugs to eat.

the Witch's Finger

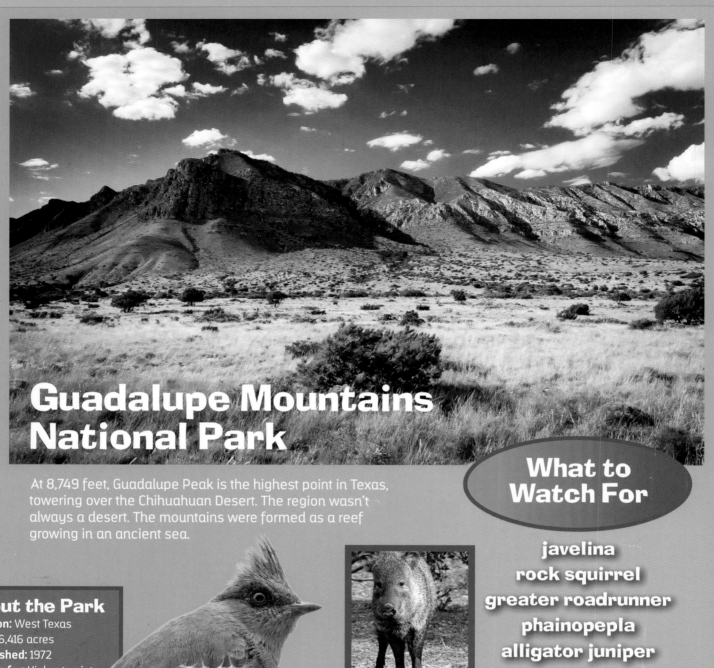

Guadalupe Mountains National Park

At 8,749 feet, Guadalupe Peak is the highest point in Texas, towering over the Chihuahuan Desert. The region wasn't always a desert. The mountains were formed as a reef growing in an ancient sea.

About the Park
Location: West Texas
Size: 86,416 acres
Established: 1972
Famous for: Highest point in Texas

phainopepla

javelina

What to Watch For

javelina
rock squirrel
greater roadrunner
phainopepla
alligator juniper

alligator juniper

greater roadrunner

Ranger Rick's
Top Thing to Do in
GUADALUPE MOUNTAINS
National Park

If you are up for a 3,000-foot climb and an 8.5-mile round-trip hike, you can walk to the "Top of Texas." Guadalupe Peak is the highest point in the state. Devil's Hall Trail requires some boulder scrambling as you explore a rocky wash. If a modest walk is more your style, try the Smith Spring Loop or the Pinery Trail.

Ranger Rick's TOP FACT About
GUADALUPE MOUNTAINS National Park

From the Chihuahuan Desert specialists and the high mountain nesters, Guadalupe Mountains National Park is home to around 300 species of birds. McKittrick Canyon is a prime location, as are William's Ranch and Guadalupe Canyon, Frijole Ranch and Smith Springs, and Pine Springs.

About the Park
Location: West Texas
Size: 801,163 acres
Established: 1944
Famous for: Remote stretch of
    the Rio Grande River in the
    Chihuahuan Desert

Big Bend National Park

A remote national park in west Texas, Big Bend has classic Chihuahuan Desert landscapes with the added bonus of isolated canyons along the Rio Grande River. It is an excellent park to explore by foot, car, horseback, or even boat. There are more species of birds, bats, and cacti in Big Bend than in any other national park.

What to Watch For

Mexican long-nosed bat
colima warbler
Big Bend slider
Big Bend gambusia (Big Bend mosquitofish)
Big Bend bluebonnets

Mexican long-nosed bat

colima warbler

Big Bend slider

Ranger Rick's
Top Thing to Do
in BIG BEND National Park

Big Bend National Park is named after a big bend in the Rio Grande River. So why not experience the river firsthand? From day trips to multiple night excursions, floating the Rio Grande is an adventure. Perhaps the easiest trip is paddling upstream from the Santa Elena Canyon Trailhead and then floating back downstream.

Ranger Rick's TOP FACT
About BIG BEND National Park

Like many of the national parks, Big Bend has stunning night skies. In fact, it has the least amount of light pollution out of all of the national parks in the lower 48 states. You've probably never seen the stars like you can from Big Bend. Perhaps you'll be able to pick out some planets or the Milky Way, too. And if you're extra lucky, you might see a shooting star!

Big Bend bluebonnets

About the Park
Location: Near Tucson, Arizona
Size: 91,440 acres
Established: 1994
Famous for: Namesake saguaro cactus

Saguaro National Park

In the United States saguaro cacti are found only in the Southwest. These cactuses grow to towering heights and are the forests of the Sonoran Desert.

What to Watch For

lesser long-nosed bat
coati
gila woodpecker
gila monster
saguaro cactus

gila woodpecker

coati

saguaro cactus

lesser long-nosed bat

gila monster

Ranger Rick's
Top Thing to Do
in SAGUARO National Park

Saguaro National Park makes a great hiking destination whether you're out for a short stroll or an epic adventure covering many miles. The Tucson Mountain District is dominated by the stately saguaro cactus forests and is representative of the lowland Sonoran Desert. The Rincon Mountain District highlights the high desert environment. As the elevation increases saguaros are replaced by oak, pine, and then fir forests the higher up you go.

desert tortoise

Ranger Rick's
TOP FACT
About SAGUARO National Park

Saguaro are the largest cacti in the country. They are slow-growing and can live up to 250 years. The don't get their signature arms until they are at least 50 years old. The cacti provide essential habitat for many animals including Gila woodpeckers, elf owls, white-winged doves, kangaroo rats, desert tortoises, and many more.

About the Park
Location: Eastern Arizona
Size: 93,533 acres
Established: 1962
Famous for: World's largest
concentration of petrified wood

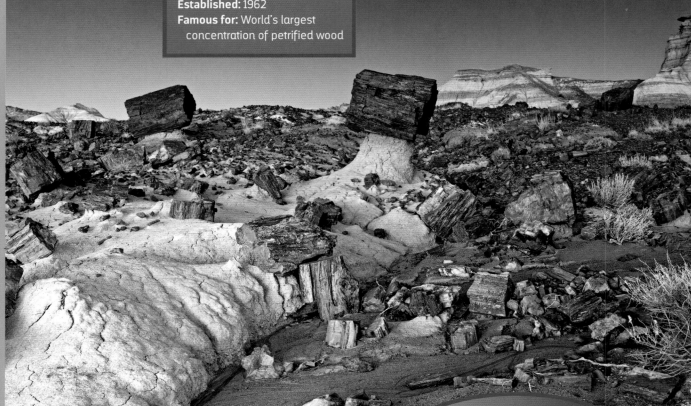

Petrified Forest National Park

Petrified wood is an accent in a varied painted desert landscape of reds, pinks, purples, yellows, and more. Historic Route 66 passes through the park, adding a bit of recent history to the park as well.

What to Watch For

coyote
black-tailed jackrabbit
evening primrose
horned lark
kingsnake

black-tailed jackrabbit

coyote

horned lark

evening primrose

Ranger Rick's Top Thing to Do
in PETRIFIED FOREST National Park

Access to much of Petrified Forest National Park is from the main park road. Stunning overlooks provide a bird's eye view, but following along on one of the many trails is the best way to experience the park. Giant Logs and Long Logs Trails showcase the petrified trees, while the Agate House Trail and Newspaper Rock Overlook highlight the area's Puebloan culture. Blue Mesa is a nice trail for hiking amongst the desert badlands.

Ranger Rick's
TOP FACT About PETRIFIED FOREST National Park

Petrified wood fossils are the most famous of the fossils in the park and also some of the largest, measuring up to 190 feet. There are numerous other plant and animals fossils, too. Some of the oldest go back over 200 million years to the Late Triassic.

About the Park
Location: Northern Arizona
Size: 1,217,403 acres
Established: 1919
Famous for: An incredible canyon along the banks of the Colorado River

Grand Canyon National Park

One of the most recognizable and popular national parks, Grand Canyon is an impressive landscape, and a World Heritage Site. The canyon itself is up to 18 miles wide and a mile deep. The Colorado River flows for 277 miles through the park, although most park visitors never make it all the way down to the water.

bighorn sheep

What to Watch For

bighorn sheep
Abert's squirrel
California condor
tarantula
pinyon & juniper forests

Abert's squirrel

Desert View Watchtower

Ranger Rick's Top 5 Things to Do in GRAND CANYON National Park

1 Hiking the Rim Trail will guide you to numerous stunning overlooks. Bright Angel Trail is a great way to hike below the rim, even if you turn back at the Upper or Lower Tunnel.

2 A more leisurely way to explore the Grand Canyon is with a mule ride. You can take a mule all the way down to Phantom Ranch at the bottom of the canyon.

3 You can also take a bike ride along the Greenway Trail.

4 Visit the Yavapai Geology Museum to fully appreciate the landscapes of the Grand Canyon.

5 The Grand Canyon has many spectacular overlooks, but only one watchtower. Climb to the top of the Desert View Watchtower near the East Entrance Station.

Ranger Rick's AMAZING FACTS
About GRAND CANYON National Park

- A Colorado River rafting trip can take as long as 18 days, but this world-class floating experience is like nothing else.

- John Wesley Powell, a one-armed Civil War veteran, led a rafting expedition down the Colorado River in 1869.

- It takes 200 miles of driving to get to the North Rim of the Grand Canyon (and it's closed off in winter), but here the Kaibab Plateau is a remote way to experience a wilder side of the Grand Canyon.

- At nearly 10 feet the wingspan of California condors is the largest of any North American landbird. These endangered vultures nest in the park as well as in parts of Utah and California.

rafting down the Colorado River

hiking along the edge of the canyon and enjoying spectacular views

10 FEET

California condor with a wing tag that lets scientists recognize individual birds

mule deer

About the Park
Location: Southeast Utah
Size: 76,519 acres
Established: 1929
Famous for: Large concentration
of natural arches

Delicate Arch

Arches National Park

You've definitely seen pictures of Arches. It's one of the most iconic national parks of the Southwest. Here, you can find more than 2,000 natural stone arches, so get those cameras ready. You'll have lots of opportunities to take amazing shots.

What to Watch For

mule deer
bighorn sheep
porcupine
western scrub jay
western collared lizard

mule deer

bighorn sheep

western collared lizard

western scrub jay

Balanced Rock

Delicate Arch

Fiery Furnace

Ranger Rick's Top 5 Things to Do in ARCHES National Park

1 Go see Delicate Arch, the most famous arch in the park. (It's so famous that it's even on the Utah license plates.) The hike is about three miles total. If you can go at dusk, you'll get awesome photos.

2 Now that you've seen the famous arch up close, go to Delicate Arch Viewpoint. This gives you an awesome view about a mile out, and it's another good photo opportunity.

3 Sign up for a Fiery Furnace guided hike. Some hikes are worth doing guided, and this is one of them. You have to be able to move, squeeze through small spaces, and drink lots of water since it gets really hot in here!

4 Get pictures of Three Penguins. This is a famous formation in the park that looks like penguins!

5 Challenge yourself to get 20 different pictures of the cool arches in the park, and then see what you think they are shaped like.

Double O Arch

Ranger Rick's
AMAZING FACTS
About ARCHES
National Park

Just how old are the formations in this park? Scientists estimate they are more than 300 million years old.

The arches can be fragile. In fact since the 1970s, more than 40 have collapsed. Remember, these arches were formed from erosion, so every year they get a tad bit weaker.

President Hoover designated this area a national monument in 1929. Then it finally became a national park in 1971.

sunrise at the needles

Canyonlands National Park

Canyonlands is an impressive network of canyons, arches, and slots. Years of erosion have left a gorgeous landscape in the Colorado Plateau. When you go, just imagine what's hidden in all those layers of rock.

pinyon jay

What to Watch For

bobcat
mule deer
white-tailed antelope ground squirrel
pinyon jay
midget-faded rattlesnake

Schafer Trail

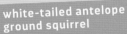
white-tailed antelope ground squirrel

bobcat

Green River

Ranger Rick's
Top Thing to Do
in CANYONLANDS
National Park

Mesa Arch hike is relatively quick and easy, and it's always a popular one. If you have some extra time, look into rafting the waters in the canyons.

learning about the park

Ranger Rick's
TOP FACT About
CANYONLANDS
National Park

The famous naturalist and author, Edward Abbey, said this about the park. It is "the most weird, wonderful, magical place on Earth—there is nothing else like it anywhere."

Mesa Arch

Capitol Reef National Park

This is the heart of the red rock area in the southwest, and Capitol Reef sure won't disappoint. When you look at the scene, it looks more like a painting than something real—definitely something to see in person!

About the Park
Location: Southern Utah
Size: 241,904 acres
Established: 1971
Famous for: Red and rugged landscape that locals referred to as a "reef"

Capitol Reef

What to Watch For

bighorn sheep
golden eagle
striped whipsnake
canyon treefrog
side-blotched lizard

side-blotched lizard

canyon treefrog

golden eagle

Ranger Rick's
Top Thing to Do
in CAPITOL REEF National Park

Go to Panorama Point. With that kind of name—panorama usually means a wide, beautiful view—you have to see if it lives up to it.

Panorama Point

the Fruita District

Ranger Rick's
TOP FACT About
CAPITOL REEF
National Park

The Fruita District is an area in the park with more than 2,500 fruit and nut trees. Not only can you get some yummy snacks (plan your visit during harvest time), but it also makes it the biggest orchard in the national park system!

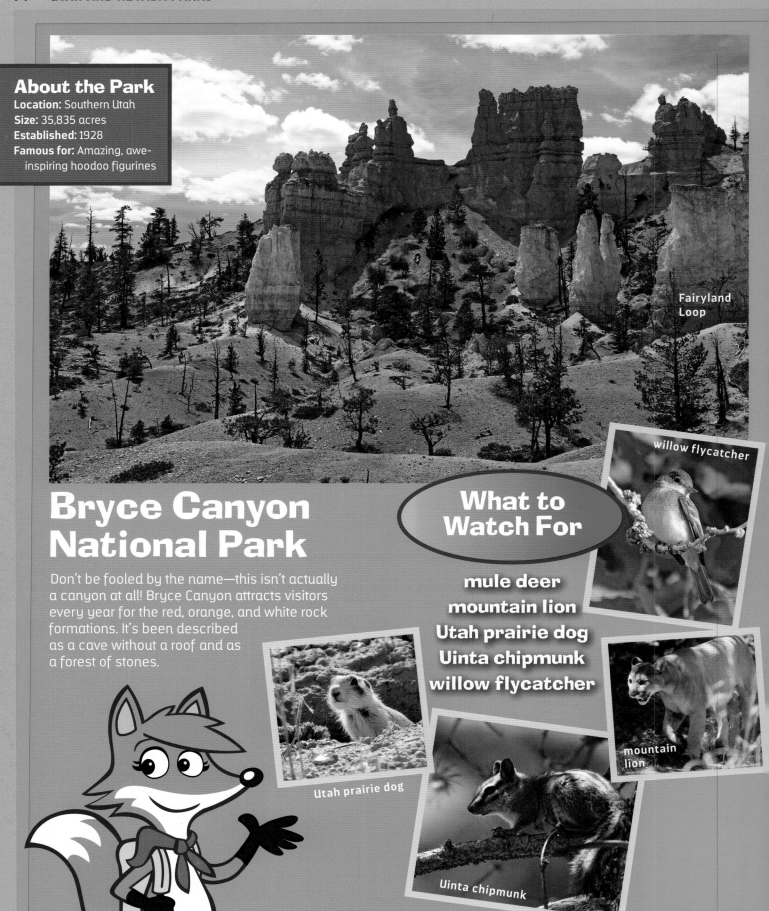

About the Park
Location: Southern Utah
Size: 35,835 acres
Established: 1928
Famous for: Amazing, awe-inspiring hoodoo figurines

Fairyland Loop

Bryce Canyon National Park

Don't be fooled by the name—this isn't actually a canyon at all! Bryce Canyon attracts visitors every year for the red, orange, and white rock formations. It's been described as a cave without a roof and as a forest of stones.

What to Watch For

mule deer
mountain lion
Utah prairie dog
Uinta chipmunk
willow flycatcher

willow flycatcher

Utah prairie dog

mountain lion

Uinta chipmunk

Bryce Amphitheater

Ranger Rick's **Top Thing to Do** in BRYCE CANYON National Park

Go visit the Bryce Amphitheater. You can find lots of trails that lead into here. This is definitely the most popular spot in the park, but it's completely worth it. You won't be able to resist taking a photo.

hoodoos

Ranger Rick's TOP FACT About BRYCE CANYON National Park

The rock formations in Bryce Canyon are called hoodoos. They came from thousands of years of erosion. Many people say they resemble humans.

About the Park

Location: Southwest Utah
Size: 146,598 acres
Established: 1919
Famous for: Stunning sandstone,
      canyons, pillars, and peaks

Court of the Patriarchs

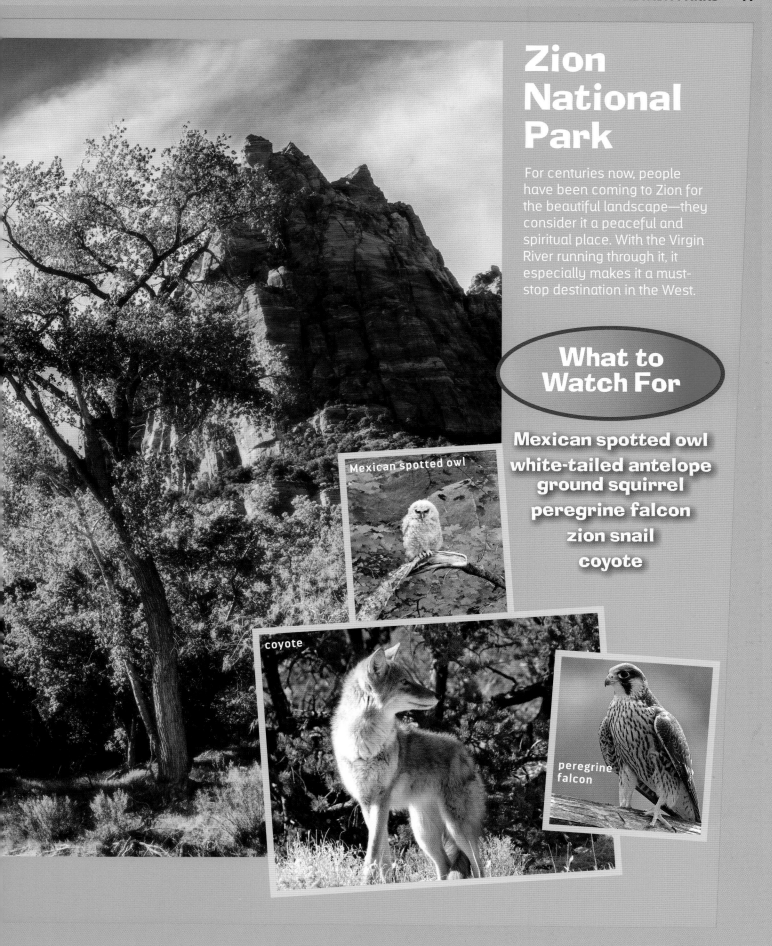

Zion National Park

For centuries now, people have been coming to Zion for the beautiful landscape—they consider it a peaceful and spiritual place. With the Virgin River running through it, it especially makes it a must-stop destination in the West.

What to Watch For

Mexican spotted owl
white-tailed antelope ground squirrel
peregrine falcon
zion snail
coyote

Mexican spotted owl

coyote

peregrine falcon

Observation Point

Ranger Rick's **Top** Things to Do in **ZION** National Park

1 Check out Angel's Landing. This hike is around 5 ½ miles, and the last half is really intense. If you don't like heights or ledges, this might not be for you. But if you like adventure, rally your family!

2 For a shorter hike, try Canyon Overlook. The view will definitely make you take a deep breath!

3 Hike through The Narrows; at least part of it. This trail goes along a deep (2,000 feet) canyon, alongside the Virgin River. Be ready to get wet if you need to go through tricky trails.

4 Drive along Kolob Canyons Road. There are plenty of places to pull off, and the views are awesome.

5 Go camping! They have some of the best campgrounds around, but reservations fill up really fast, so sign up early.

The Narrows

The Virgin River

Ranger Rick's AMAZING FACTS About ZION National Park

● Records show that giant sloths, camels, and mammoths used to be in this area about 12,000 years ago.

● This is considered a holy area. In fact, the name Zion is Hebrew for Jerusalem. Many people come here, seeking peace, every year.

● The Virgin River is one of the steepest streams in North America. It drops more than 50 feet per mile in this area.

About the Park
Location: Eastern Nevada
Size: 77,180 acres
Established: 1986
Famous for: The basin formations throughout the area

Wheeler Peak

Great Basin National Park

The Great Basin region is a huge area, which extends from California to Utah. This park is located near Wheeler Peak, a 13,000-foot mountain. Be sure to admire these unique formations of land where rivers and streams drain.

What to Watch For

bristlecone pine
pygmy rabbit
American badger
common raven
western skink

common raven

bristlecone pine

American badger

pygmy rabbit

Ranger Rick's
Top Thing to Do
in GREAT BASIN National Park

Great Basin has everything from sagebrush plains to mountain peaks. It also has Lehman Caves, so go spelunking (which is also called caving). You can sign up for two different tours—the Lodge Room Tour or the Grand Palace Tour. This second one is where you'll be able to see the famous Parachute Shield formation.

Ranger Rick's
TOP FACT
About GREAT BASIN
National Park

During the 1960s, a graduate student went through this area because he was searching for the world's oldest tree. He found Prometheus, which was nearly 5,000 years old. Similar bristlecone pines are throughout this area as well.

Lehman Caves

Wheeler Peak

About the Park
Location: Southern California
Size: 789,745 acres
Established: 1994
Famous for: Joshua trees that are native to the park

joshua trees

Joshua Tree National Park

This park is formed at the edge of two deserts, the Mojave and the Colorado. This fact alone makes Joshua Tree a fascinating place to visit because you can find a lot of desert plants and animals here that you won't find anywhere else.

What to Watch For

**Gambel's quail
cactus wren
desert tortoise
western chuckwalla
joshua tree**

cactus wren

desert tortoise

Gambel's quail

western chuckwalla

Skull Rock

Ranger Rick's
Top Thing to Do
in JOSHUA TREE
National Park

This park is really well known among rock climbers, and there are many formations to check out. One that you'll want just to look at (but not climb) is the famous Skull Rock. The giant rock resembles a decomposing skull.

learning the history of the park

Joshua tree during sunset

Ranger Rick's **TOP FACT**
About JOSHUA TREE National Park

The famous trees here, Joshua trees, are part of the agave family. They look a little strange (some say they look like trees from a Dr. Seuss book). For years Native Americans have worked the tough leaves of the Joshua Trees into baskets and sandals.

COTTONWOOD SPRINGS
PARKING AREA
.4 MI.

MASTODON PEAK
LOOP TRAILHEAD
VIA LOST PALMS TRAIL 2.8 MI.

LOST PALMS
OASIS
4.1 MI.

CAMPGROUND LOOPS
A&B

MASTODON PEAK 24 MI.
LOOP

LOST PALMS 45 MI.
OASIS

Channel Islands National Park

When you're in southern California, it can be hard to imagine there are nature areas nearby. This is exactly the case with the Channel Islands. You can drive to mainland visitor centers, but you'll have to access the islands by boat or plane. It's worth the extra effort.

What to Watch For

island fox
island deer mouse
pacific gray whale
California sea lion
island scrub-jay

California sea lions

island fox

island scrub-jay

Ranger Rick's
Top Thing to Do
in CHANNEL ISLANDS
National Park

Since these are islands, you'll have to find a good way to get there first. Don't worry about having a car once you get on the islands, because car transportation isn't allowed. Make sure you find a good tour company to take you to Anacapa Island. It's one of the smaller islands, but home to Anacapa Island Light Station as well as large flocks of western gulls and brown pelicans.

Anacapa Island Light Station

natural bridge

Ranger Rick's
TOP FACT About
CHANNEL ISLANDS
National Park

You can actually find eight islands in this grouping, but only five are included as designated National lands, including Santa Barbara, Anacapa, Santa Cruz, Santa Rosa, and San Miguel.

gray whale

Pinnacles National Park

This park was formed roughly 23 million years ago by multiple volcano eruptions. Though the volcanoes are now gone, it is still a very unique landscape, which includes woodlands, canyons, unique rock formations, and caves.

What to Watch For

black-tailed deer
acorn woodpecker
California condor
California red-legged frog
acmon blue butterfly

acorn woodpecker

California red-legged frog

black-tailed deer

Ranger Rick's
Top Thing to Do
in PINNACLES
National Park

Bear Gulch Cave and Balconies Cave are worth exploring. These unique talus caves were formed when large boulders tumbled into narrow canyons. The rocks piled up, but many gaps and openings remained. You might be lucky enough to see some of the caves' many species of bats. Birding is also popular at this park, so grab your binoculars.

Bear Gulch cave

California condor

acmon blue butterfly

Ranger Rick's
TOP FACT About
PINNACLES
National Park

This is one of our newest national parks. It started as a national monument, dedicated by President Theodore Roosevelt in 1908. In 2012, Congress officially designated it to be a national park, and in January of 2013, President Barack Obama officially signed it into law.

About the Park

Location: Along California and Nevada border
Size: 3,372,402 acres
Established: 1994
Famous for: The lowest point in the United States

Dante's View

Death Valley National Park

This national park is filled with extreme conditions. It's incredibly dry. It's really hot. And it's the lowest point in the United States. Because of these factors, it might not seem like there's a lot to see or do, but that's not the case at all. You'll be surprised just how much diversity you can find here.

What to Watch For

black-tailed jackrabbit
bighorn sheep
greater roadrunner
desert tortoise
Mojave desert sidewinder

Mojave Desert sidewinder

greater roadrunner

desert tortoise

Zabriskie Point

Ranger Rick's Top Things to Do in DEATH VALLEY National Park

Scotty's castle

1. Hike Dante's Ridge Trail. The road to get to this trail is long and steep, but the hike you can do is worth the drive. You can see the Black Mountains along the way to Dante's View.

2. Stop at Zabriskie Point, one of the most famous spots in the park. Visitors come here to see the impressive landscape, which is unique because of all the erosion in this area.

3. Drive through Titus Canyon Road. This canyon includes mountains, cool rock formations, rare plants, wildlife sightings, and a ghost town!

4. Swing by a place called "The Racetrack," which is a dry lakebed. The scene definitely resembles what most think of as Death Valley. It also has moving rocks, which no one can seem to explain why.

5. Visit Scotty's Castle. This is a house and museum that explains the story of Walter Scott or "Death Valley Scotty" who was a bit of a con-artist in the 1920s and 30s.

bighorn sheep

Ranger Rick's AMAZING FACTS About DEATH VALLEY National Park

- This park is actually the largest in the lower 48 states, sitting at more than 3 million acres.

- Summers are hot and dry, just like you might expect. Temperatures are consistently over 100°F and easily reach upwards of 120°F. (Psst—summer might not be the best time to visit!)

- Badwater Basin is located in the park, which is the lowest elevation in North America at 282 feet below sea level.

- The highest point in the lower 48 states is also in Death Valley—it's Mount Whitney and it stands at 14,505 feet.

The Racetrack

ELEVATION SEA LEVEL

Sequoia & Kings Canyon National Parks

Just a couple hours from Yosemite, Sequoia and Kings Canyon are worth the detour. While they have their own entrances, they back up to one another by the Sierra Nevada. Even though they are two parks, the National Park Service administers them together since they are so close.

What to Watch For

black bear
bighorn sheep
California kingsnake
California newt
giant sequoia

About the Park

Location: Southeast of Yosemite in eastern California
Size: 865,257 acres
Established: 1890 (Sequoia) and 1940 (Kings Canyon)
Famous for: The giant sequoia trees, including General Sherman and General Grant

black bear

California newt

bighorn sheep

California kingsnake

General Sherman

Ranger Rick's **Top Thing to Do** in SEQUOIA & KINGS CANYON National Park

There's just no way around it—you have to go and see the giant sequoia trees. You can find 75 different tree groves in the two parks with more than 15,000 trees. If you have time, be sure to check out the caves in the park, too. (There are more than 250 caves.)

Ranger Rick's **TOP FACT** About SEQUOIA & KINGS CANYON National Park

General Sherman, in Sequoia, is the world's largest tree, and General Grant, in Kings Canyon, is the world's second largest tree. This definitely makes them worth visiting!

Glacier Point

About the Park
Location: Eastern California
Size: 761,268 acres
Established: 1890
Famous for: Inspiring rock and waterfall landscapes

Yosemite National Park

This is one of the most popular parks in America. Located in California and only a short distance from Nevada, it offers a huge variety of things to do and see. Some people come for the giant sequoias, others come for the amazing rock climbing, and everyone comes for the great views.

What to Watch For

black bear
California ground squirrel
Steller's jay
Yosemite toad
sierra garter snake

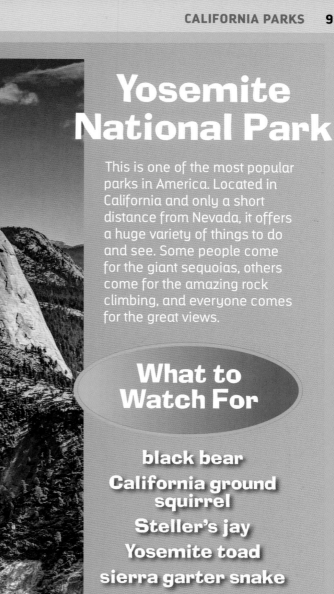

black bear

Yosemite toad

sierra garter snake

California ground squirrel

Ranger Rick's Top 5 Things to Do in YOSEMITE National Park

El Capitan

1 Go to Mariposa Grove and hike the trail (1.6 miles) to see the famous giant sequoia tree, Grizzly Giant. Don't forget to take a picture, trying to wrap your arms around it.

2 Hike to Glacier Point, which has one of the best views of the park. You can see Yosemite Valley, Yosemite Falls, and the Half Domes, which is featured on back of the California state quarter.

3 Go on one of the most famous hikes in Yosemite, Mist Trail, where you can climb 1,000 feet to Vernal Fall and another 1,900 feet to Nevada Fall. While you're in this area, don't forget to stop by the Happy Isles Nature Center.

4 Climb, climb, climb at the hiking trails of Gaylor Lakes. This hiking area isn't as popular as others directly in Yosemite Valley, which is awesome if you don't like lots of crowds. The first part of this 3-mile hike is very steep, but the views are spectacular and it gets a lot easier after that.

5 Put your climbing shoes on to try out the rock-climbing wall at Tenaya Lodge. Yosemite is famous for attracting rock climbers of all skills. Once you give it a try yourself, head down to the El Capitan Meadow and watch the expert rock climbers at work.

grizzly giant

Ranger Rick's AMAZING FACTS About YOSEMITE National Park

● Ansel Adams, one of the most famous photographers in the world, was only 14 when he first got interested in Yosemite.

● El Capitan is the biggest formation (or some would say mountain) of granite in the entire world.

● Yosemite Falls is the tallest waterfall in North America at nearly 2,500 feet. It mostly flows from melted snow, so the best time to see the falls are in spring through early summer.

Stellar's jay

Yosemite Falls

About the Park
Location: Northeast California
Size: 106,372 acres
Established: 1916
Famous for: The largest plug dome volcano in the world

Lassen Volcanic National Park

You can find active volcanoes right here in Lassen Volcanic National Park. Just look for the boiling mud pots, hot springs, and steam. This national park is especially cool because it's one of the only places in the world where you can see all four types of volcanoes—plug dome, shield, cinder cone, and strato.

What to Watch For

red fox

golden-mantled ground squirrel

white-headed woodpecker

California tortoiseshell butterfly

pacific treefrog

white-headed woodpecker

pacific treefrog

golden-mantled ground squirrel

California tortoiseshell butterfly

Boiling Springs Lake

Ranger Rick's Top Thing to Do in LASSEN VOLCANIC National Park

Spend the day at Manzanita Lake, which is located in the northwest corner of the park. It has some of the best views of the Lassen Peak. Plus, you can spend the day swimming, kayaking, and enjoying the water if the weather is good.

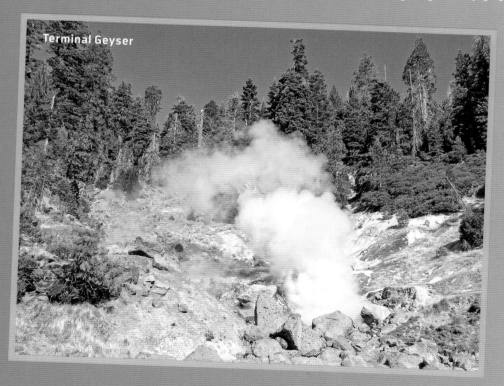

Terminal Geyser

Ranger Rick's TOP FACT About LASSEN VOLCANIC National Park

This park actually started as two national monuments, including Cinder Cone and Lassen Peak. President Theodore Roosevelt designated them in 1907, and it led to their protection for many years.

foothill trail

Redwood National Park

Definitely go to Redwood National Park to see the famous redwoods, which are also known as some of the tallest trees on earth, but then stay to see all the other great trees, plants, and nature found throughout the forests. The variety and diversity can't be missed.

What to Watch For

Roosevelt elk
California sea lion
marbled murrelet
banana slug
redwood

California sea lions

banana slug

marbled murrelet

Roosevelt elk

About the Park

Location: Northern California
Size: 112,512
Established: 1968
Famous for: Redwood trees, which are some of the oldest and tallest trees in the world

Ranger Rick's
Top Thing to Do
in REDWOOD National Park

Hike Lady Bird Johnson Grove, which is a short hike near the Kuchel Visitor Center. If you walk the grove here and still have time, stop by the Klamath River Overlook for gorgeous views and a sniff of the salty sea air.

hiking "through" the forest

driving "through" the forest

TUNNEL LOG

Ranger Rick's
TOP FACT
About REDWOOD National Park

Much of the redwood forests have been logged over the years. Back in 1850, the redwood forests covered more than 2 million acres of California. Today, less than 40,000 acres are left.

About the Park
Location: Southern Oregon
Size: 183,224 acres
Established: 1902
Famous for: Deep lake with clear blue waters

Crater Lake National Park

The history of Crater Lake is fascinating. It was the volcanic eruption of Mount Mazama that created the huge hole in the earth around 8,000 years ago. Meanwhile, gorgeous cliffs of 4,000 feet high surround the big crater, making it a truly spectacular view.

coastal tailed frog

What to Watch For

bald eagle
northern spotted owl
bull trout
mazama newt
coastal tailed frog

bald eagle

northern spotted owl

Crater Lake Lodge

Ranger Rick's **Top Thing to Do** in CRATER LAKE National Park

The water is really cold—usually only about 55 degrees—so don't expect to do a lot of swimming. But you should still stop and see the lake. You also might want to check out Rim Village. It's one of the only roads that lead to a scenic view of the lake.

bull trout

Ranger Rick's **TOP FACT** About CRATER LAKE National Park

This is definitely the deepest lake in the United States. At the deepest point, Crater Lake goes down 1,943 feet.

About the Park
Location: Central Washington
Size: 235,625 acres
Established: 1899
Famous for: Stunning Mount Rainier

Mount Rainier National Park

This famous national park is centered around Mount Rainier, the 14,410-foot volcano, which can be seen from hundreds of miles away, including from Seattle. It was the fifth national park designated in the United States, and it's in the top 10 of most visited.

What to Watch For

black-tailed deer
Douglas squirrel
American marten
Steller's jay
common raven

American marten

black-tailed deer

Steller's jay

Douglas squirrel

common raven

Ranger Rick's Top 5 Things to Do in MOUNT RAINIER National Park

1 Visit Paradise—the area where most climbers will start their journey to climb Mount Rainier. This area receives more than 600 inches of snow a year, so some people call it one of the snowiest places on Earth. If you like this, visit in winter. If you'd rather see wildflowers, go in summer.

2 Hike Comet Falls Trailhead almost 4 miles in, and you'll be rewarded with gorgeous, 300-foot falls.

3 Stop to do some hiking at Skyline Loop. It can be challenging (more than 15,000 feet elevation gain), but the sights along the way are amazing.

4 Drive Sunrise Road. It's the only peak that you can climb by car, and the views are great. Start early if you can.

5 Go to Mount Rainier during the summer and stop to take wildflower photos. The Paradise and Sunrise areas are great choices to see if you can get photos of 20 different wildflowers. (The park is actually home to more than 100.)

Ranger Rick's AMAZING FACTS About MOUNT RAINIER National Park

- Roughly 10,000 people try to climb (or summit) Mount Rainier each year. Not all are successful, though—it's a tough climb. Only 25-50% of people make it.

- If you do reach the top of Mount Rainier, you can look down and see 26 glaciers covering the area. This includes the Carbon Glacier, on the north side. It's the thickest glacier (700 feet) in the United States.

- On a clear day, you can see Mount Rainier for about 100 miles in all directions.

About the Park
Location: Central Washington
Size: 504,781 acres
Established: 1968
Famous for: Hiking trails, which lead to spectacular views

Northern Cascades National Park

Forests, glaciers, and lakes—you'll find all three of these in the North Cascades National Park. This area is one of the most popular for hikers. You'll find dozens of great trails to check out, and you can spot a mountain goat along the way.

What to Watch For

black-tailed deer
long-toed salamander
wolverine
pika
bald eagle

wolverine

long-toed salamander

black-tailed deer

Ranger Rick's
Top Thing to Do
in NORTHERN CASCADES
National Park

Drive the North Cascades Highway. This highway goes along the Cascade Mountains from east to west, and it really gives you a great look at this area. So put those phones and electronics down and watch out the window!

north cascades highway

Ranger Rick's
TOP FACT About
NORTHERN CASCADES
National Park

The mountains here are actually named after all the waterfalls in the area, which form a natural barrier around the mountains.

pika

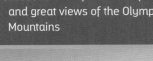

About the Park

Location: Olympic Peninsula of northwest Washington
Size: 922,651 acres
Established: 1938
Famous for: Temperate rain forests and great views of the Olympic Mountains

Olympic National Park

Don't overlook this park just because it's in the far northwest part of the United States. There is so much to see in this enormous park, between the famous Roosevelt elk and Mount Olympus, so it's best to plan on staying for a few days if possible.

What to Watch For

Roosevelt elk
Olympic yellow-pine chipmunk
sea otter
Olympic marmot
Olympic torrent salamander

sea otters

Olympic marmot

Olympic yellow-pine chipmunk

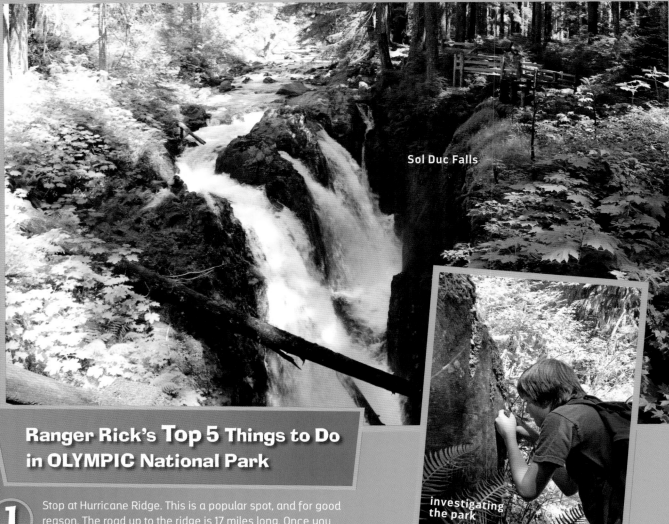

Sol Duc Falls

investigating the park

Ranger Rick's **Top 5** Things to Do in OLYMPIC National Park

1 Stop at Hurricane Ridge. This is a popular spot, and for good reason. The road up to the ridge is 17 miles long. Once you reach the top, it's a beautiful view where you can also get great pictures of Mount Olympus.

2 Visit the Hoh Rain Forest on the west side of the park. This area sees about 150 inches of rain a year. It's truly one of the best temperate rain forests in the United States.

3 Grab your bathing suits and stop at Sol Duc. This area has three natural hot springs you can stop at for a hot soak, and you can hike the area to see the Sol Duc Falls as well.

4 Stop for a hike or dip in the waters of Lake Crescent. This beautiful lake is hard to miss if you're driving into the park from the north. It was carved by glaciers 12,000 years ago, and the scenery is spectacular.

5 Stop at Rialto Beach. The shorelines in this area of Washington are gorgeous, offering a completely different type of shoreline than the East Coast or farther south in the west. You'll definitely want to explore the ocean life.

Ranger Rick's **AMAZING FACTS** About OLYMPIC National Park

- The largest herd of wild Roosevelt elk lives right here in the park.

- Olympic National Park is home to many animals that you can't find anywhere else in the world including the Olympic marmot, Olympic torrent salamander, and Olympic grasshopper.

- Captain John Meares named Mount Olympus in 1788 because he thought it was worthy of the Greek gods (and legend says they live on Mount Olympus in Greece).

- Mount Olympus stands 7,980 feet tall.

About the Park
Location: The big island of Hawai'i
Size: 330,000 acres
Established: 1916
Famous for: The unique volcanic landscape

Hawai'i Volcanoes National Park

This national park has a little bit of everything, including fire, water, rock, sand, rainforest, desert, and the world's most active volcano—the Kilauea Volcano.

'i'iwi honeycreeper

Hawaiian silversword

hawksbill sea turtle

What to Watch For

'i'iwi honeycreeper
Hawaiian petrel ('ua'u)
hawksbill sea turtle (honu'ea)
red lehua ('ohi'a lehua)
Hawaiian silversword

red lehua

Ranger Rick's Top Things to Do in HAWAI'I VOLCANOES National Park

1 Hike the 4-mile Kilauea Iki Trail. This will give you an up-close look at an active volcano. If you make a loop back out on the hike, you'll even go through a rain forest.

2 Take the Crater Rim Drive. They call this a "drive-in" volcano because you really are circling the Kilauea Crater. Chain of Craters Road is another driving path not too far away.

3 Check out Pu'u Loa Petroglyphs Trails. This is at the end of Chain of Craters Road. You can find more than 20,000 symbols carved into rocks.

4 Walk through the Thurston Lava Tube. This won't take you long, but it's really cool to see. This tube was created as layers of lava cooled. It really makes you feel like you're in a volcano!

5 Hit the Ka'u Desert Trail where you can look for fossilized footprints.

entrance to a Lava Tube

Lava Tube

Kilauea Crater

Ranger Rick's
AMAZING FACTS About
HAWAI'I VOLCANOES
National Park

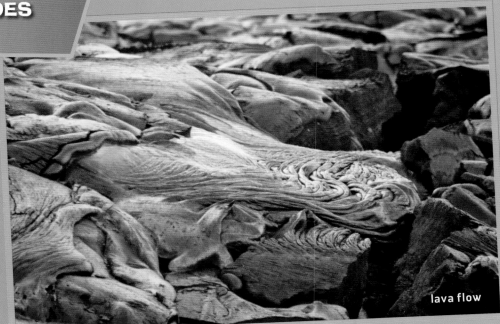

- The five volcanoes that make up the island include Kohala, Mauna Kea, Hualalai, Mauna Loa, and Kilauea.

- The lava flow of Kilauea has added more than 550 acres of land to this island. Though much of the lava goes into the ocean, this number is bound to keep growing in the future.

- Mauna Loa is actually the earth's largest mountain, but you wouldn't know it since about 18,000 feet of it is below the water. It still rises 13,679 feet above sea level.

lava flow

About the Park
Location: Maui, Hawaii
Size: 29,094 acres
Established: 1916
Famous for: Two very diverse
landscapes in one area

Haleakala National Park

It can really feel like you're in a different world (or a different planet) when you're in Haleakala National Park. It has very diverse landscapes in two distinct regions. The first is the Haleakala Summit that looks like a barren planet. The second is Lower Kipahula, which is a robust rainforest.

What to Watch For

Hawaiian hoary bat ('ope'ape'a)
monk seal
Hawaiian goose (nene)
Maui parrotbill (kiwikiu)
happy face spider

happy face spider

Hawaiian hoary bat

monk seal

nene

Ranger Rick's
Top Thing to Do
in HALEAKALA National Park

Drive up to Haleakala Summit, the island's highest peak at 10,023 feet. Short hikes to check out near the summit include Leleiwi Overlook and Hosmer's Grove Nature Trail. Also, if you're into birds, take time to make a reservation at Waikamoi Preserve.

Ranger Rick's TOP FACT
About HALEAKALA National Park

This is an area with lots of endangered species. In fact, it's home to more than any other national park in the United States.

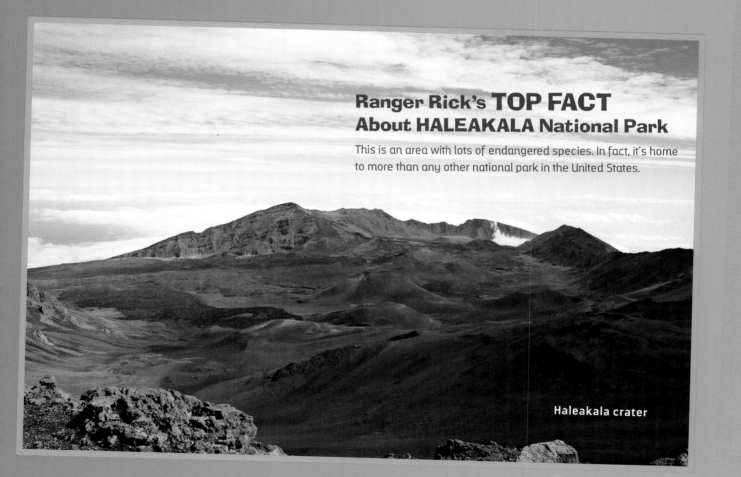

Haleakala crater

About the Park

Location: 2,300 miles southwest of Hawai'i
Size: 9,000 acres
Established: 1988
Famous for: One of the wildest national parks you can visit

Si'u Point Trail

National Park of American Samoa

Covering a portion of three islands, the National Park of American Samoa is south of the equator. It protects rare plants and animals. The park is also a showcase of traditional Samoan culture.

What to Watch For

Samoan fruit bat
humpback whale
hawksbill sea turtle
pacific slender-toed gecko
white-collared kingfisher

humpback whales

hawksbill sea turtle

white-collared kingfisher

Pago Pago Harbor

Pola Island Trail

Ranger Rick's **Top Thing to Do** in NATIONAL PARK OF AMERICAN SAMOA

You don't really go to this national park for a day trip. Make the most of it if you go. Visit the rainforests, go to the beaches, and take in the traditional Samoan culture, which is found around much of the islands.

Ranger Rick's **TOP FACT** About NATIONAL PARK OF AMERICAN SAMOA

Samoan culture is present throughout the park. The word Samoa translates to "sacred earth" and the park, along with the people of American Samoa, protects the "fa'asamoa" or the customs, beliefs, and traditions of Samoan culture that date back 3,000 years.

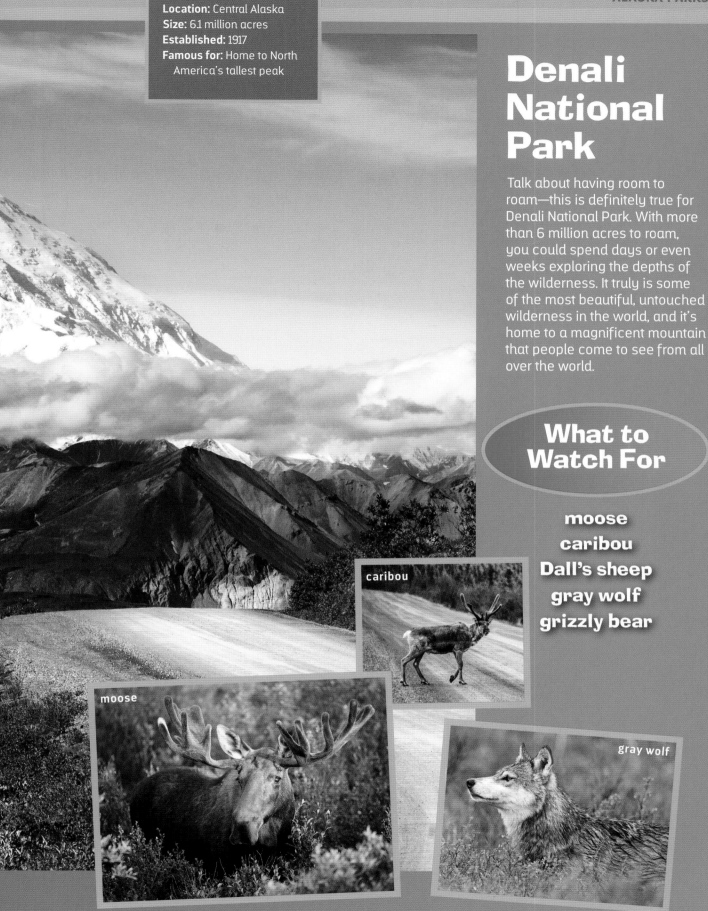

About the Park

Location: Central Alaska
Size: 6.1 million acres
Established: 1917
Famous for: Home to North America's tallest peak

Denali National Park

Talk about having room to roam—this is definitely true for Denali National Park. With more than 6 million acres to roam, you could spend days or even weeks exploring the depths of the wilderness. It truly is some of the most beautiful, untouched wilderness in the world, and it's home to a magnificent mountain that people come to see from all over the world.

What to Watch For

moose
caribou
Dall's sheep
gray wolf
grizzly bear

caribou

moose

gray wolf

Dall's sheep

riding a dogsled

Ranger Rick's Top Things to Do in DENALI National Park

1 Go to Denali at least once when there's still snow on the ground. The cross-country skiing and snowshoeing is an awesome experience. You could also ride along by dog sled!

2 You'll have to time it just right, but hire a guide or go on a fishing excursion for salmon in the lakes and streams of Denali. You can find great fishing in just about every part of this park.

3 Check out the Murie Science Learning Center. It's a true treasure in the park. The center conducts research and education programs and pretty much always has something going on.

4 Visit Talkeetna. It's the closest town to Denali, and it's got great charm while offering beautiful views of the mountain.

5 Go through the park on the Denali Star Train. This is a good way to just sit back and enjoy all the amazing scenery of the park.

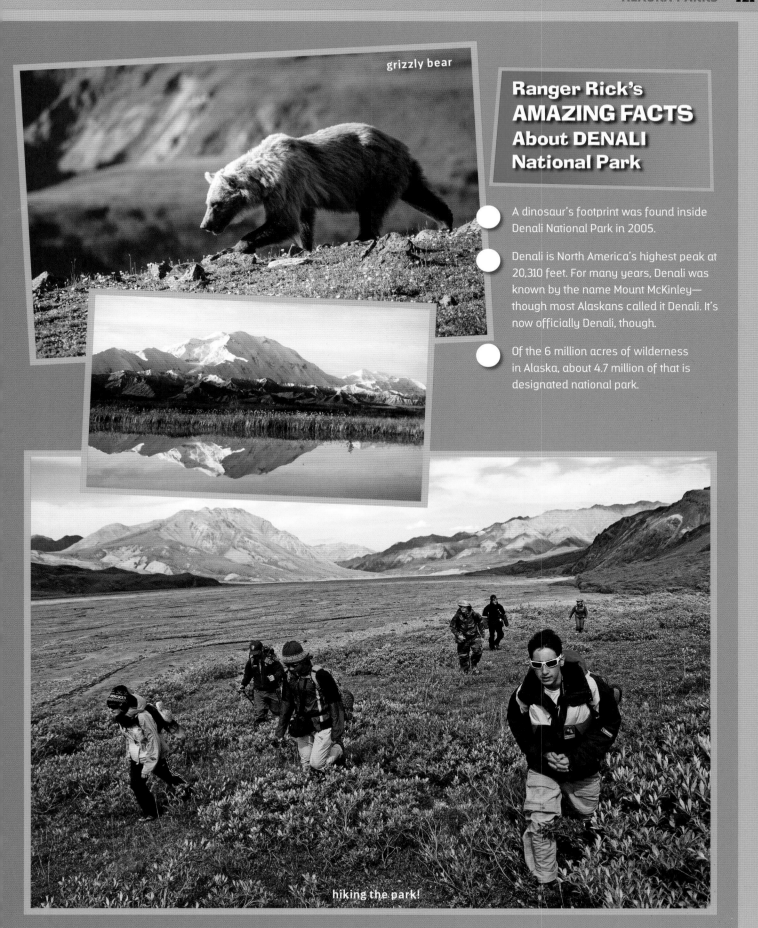

grizzly bear

Ranger Rick's
AMAZING FACTS
About DENALI
National Park

A dinosaur's footprint was found inside Denali National Park in 2005.

Denali is North America's highest peak at 20,310 feet. For many years, Denali was known by the name Mount McKinley—though most Alaskans called it Denali. It's now officially Denali, though.

Of the 6 million acres of wilderness in Alaska, about 4.7 million of that is designated national park.

hiking the park!

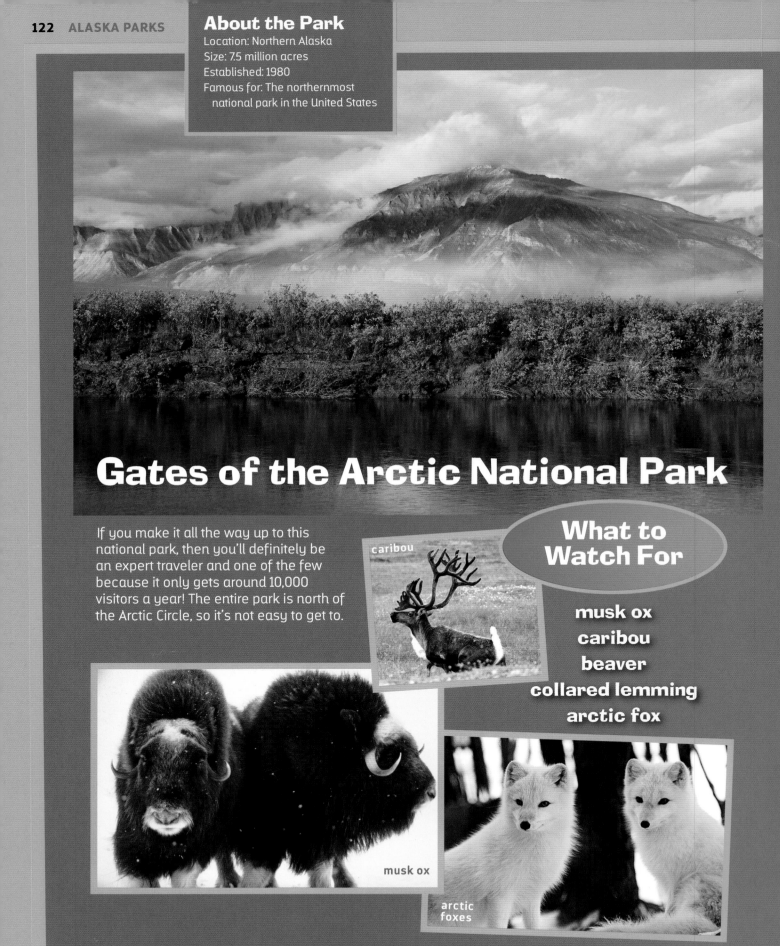

Gates of the Arctic National Park

If you make it all the way up to this national park, then you'll definitely be an expert traveler and one of the few because it only gets around 10,000 visitors a year! The entire park is north of the Arctic Circle, so it's not easy to get to.

caribou

What to Watch For

musk ox
caribou
beaver
collared lemming
arctic fox

musk ox

arctic foxes

Ranger Rick's
Top Thing to Do
in GATES OF THE ARCTIC
National Park

Go for the famous northern lights. This is definitely one of the best places in the world to see the gorgeous northern lights. So plan your trip around this. Luckily, since it's so far north, you'll have a decent chance of seeing them most of the year.

Northern Lights

Noatak River

Ranger Rick's
TOP FACT About
GATES OF THE ARCTIC
National Park

The park has the Continental Divide running through it. This means that drainages for both the Atlantic and Pacific Ocean run through here. So when the snow melts, some water ends up in the east and some in the west.

About the Park
Location: Northwest Alaska
Size: 1.7 million acres
Established: 1980
Famous for: Gorgeous scenery and sand dunes

caribou swimming

Kobuk Valley National Park

Get ready to be surprised with this park. First of all, it's 25 miles north of the Arctic Circle—pretty extreme! Second, it's also known for the Great Kobuk Sand Dunes. You probably didn't imagine sand dunes being so far north, but they are here!

What to Watch For

arctic ground squirrel
musk ox
caribou
sheefish
Kobuk locoweed

Kobuk locoweed

arctic ground squirrel

students enjoying the dunes

air taxi

sand dunes

Ranger Rick's
Top Thing to Do
in KOBUK VALLEY
National Park

Go see the dunes! You have three big sections to choose from, including the Great Kobuk Sand Dunes, Little Kobuk Sand Dunes, and the Hunt River Dunes.

Ranger Rick's
TOP FACT About
KOBUK VALLEY
National Park

You won't find any roads into this Alaskan National Park, and for this reason, it's actually one of the least visited parks in the national system. You can get here by foot, dogsled, snowmobile, or an air taxi (which is a small airplane).

About the Park
Location: Southern Alaska
Size: 2.6 million acres
Established: 1980
Famous for: Sockeye salmon

Lake Clark National Park

You will find so much in this national park-it's like all the best parts of Alaska rolled into one. It includes mountains, rainforests, volcanoes, glaciers, salmon fishing, wildlife sightings, and more. You can't reach it by road though. Instead you'll have to visit in a small plane or a boat.

What to Watch For

Canada lynx
wolverine
bald eagle
dolly varden
sockeye salmon

Canada lynx

bald eagle

wolverine

dolly varden

sockeye salmon

Ranger Rick's
Top Thing to Do
in LAKE CLARK
National Park

In an area that is known for and relies on its salmon, you have to go salmon fishing! You can go on your own, but consider hiring a guide. They'll know exactly where to take you.

Ranger Rick's
TOP FACT About
LAKE CLARK
National Park

This is such a big salmon area because the Kvichak River is the world's most active watershed for sockeye salmon. So the next time you see salmon in the store or at a restaurant, it just might have come from this area in Alaska.

Valley of Ten Thousand Smokes

Katmai National Park

Located on the Alaskan Peninsula, Katmai National Park is home to nearly 20 volcanoes. It gets its name from an enormous volcano called Mount Katmai.

What to Watch For

brown bear
red fox
northern fur seal
white-crowned sparrow
sockeye salmon

red fox

About the Park
Location: Southern Alaska
Size: 3.6 million acres
Established: 1980
Famous for: Spawning salmon and grizzly bears

northern fur seals

white-crowned sparrow

Brooks Falls

Ranger Rick's **Top Thing to Do** in **KATMAI National Park**

This national park is a great place to see Alaskan brown bears. One of the best places is Brooks Falls, so go here to watch the bears coming to fish. If you can't make it to the park, you can still watch the action on the Katmai webcam.

A brown bear enjoying a sockeye salmon

Ranger Rick's **TOP FACT** About KATMAI National Park

This park is famous for a 1912 eruption of Novarupta. This eruption formed an area called Ten Thousand Smokes. This area is still there today, and it's filled with ash from that eruption.

About the Park
Location: Southcentral Alaska
Size: 669,983 acres
Established: 1980
Famous for: The wildness of Alaska, meeting the sea

Bear Glacier

Kenai Fjords National Park

Kenai Fjords is the place where mountains, oceans, and ice come together. It is also home to an impressive diversity of wildlife, both on the land and in the sea.

What to Watch For

mountain goat
Steller's sea lion
pacific white-sided dolphin
black oystercatcher
horned puffin

black oystercatcher

Steller's sea lions

horned puffins

Ranger Rick's
Top Thing to Do
in KENAI FJORDS
National Park

Go to Exit Glacier. It's the only part of the park you can access by road, and it'll give you the chance to see an active glacier. You can find some good hiking trails in this area, too.

Exit Glacier

pacific white-sided dolphins

Ranger Rick's **TOP FACT**
About KENAI FJORDS National Park

The park is named for the fjords (pronounced *fyohrds*). Fjords are inlets of the sea between long and steep cliffs. They are created by erosion as glaciers scrape the land when advancing (growing) and retreating (shrinking).

About the Park
Location: Eastern Alaska
Size: 8 million acres
Established: 1980
Famous for: Volcanoes and huge mountains

Mount Wrangell

Wrangell-St. Elias National Park

Even by Alaska standards, Wrangle-St. Elias National Park is remote and wild. It is an incredible place to visit, especially if you enjoy mountains, volcanoes, and wildlife.

What to Watch For

Dall's sheep
moose
beaver
trumpeter swan
sockeye salmon

trumpeter swans

moose

Dall's sheep

Kennecott mines

Ranger Rick's
Top Thing to Do in
WRANGELL-ST. ELIAS
National Park

Go to the Kennecott Mines. This is actually a National Historic Landmark. Not only is it cool to see, but you can also learn all about 20th century copper mining.

Ranger Rick's TOP FACT About
WRANGELL-ST. ELIAS National Park

This park is fascinating because two large forces of nature have shaped it—volcanoes and glaciers. It still has active volcanoes. Plus, it is home to Mount St. Elias, the second highest point in the United States at 18,000 feet.

Mount St. Elias

Johns Hopkins glacier

Glacier Bay National Park

From the icy waters to the fields of ice, the shades of blue in Glacier Bay National Park are fantastic. It is amazing to see up close and personal what the glaciers have done over the years, and to still see them today.

tufted puffin

What to Watch For

sea otter
Steller's sea lion
Dall's porpoise
orca
tufted puffin

sea otter

orcas

Steller's sea lion

Johns Hopkins Inlet

Ranger Rick's **Top Thing to Do** in **GLACIER BAY** National Park

Go see the glaciers one day—after all, they help make the park famous. Then the next day, go see the temperate rainforests. Many people don't even realize there are rain forests in Alaska, but there are and they're really cool to see.

Ranger Rick's **TOP FACT** About **GLACIER BAY** National Park

You won't find any roads into this park, but people still visit. In fact, roughly half a million people come each year by cruise ship! The marine environments of the park are home to many of the coolest critters, too.

Dall's porpoises

More Information

National Seashores and Lakeshores

A handful of seashores and lakeshores have been designated as national protected areas, which are run by the National Park Service. They are definitely worth a stop on your next roadtrip, so make note of where they are located.

SEASHORES

Assateague Island National Seashore, Maryland and Virginia
Canaveral National Seashore, Florida
Cape Cod National Seashore, Massachusetts
Cape Hatteras National Seashore, North Carolina
Cape Lookout National Seashore, North Carolina
Cumberland Island National Seashore, Georgia
Fire Island National Seashore, New York
Gulf Islands National Seashore, Florida and Mississippi
Padre Island National Seashore, Texas
Point Reyes National Seashore, California

LAKESHORES

Apostle Island National Lakeshore, Wisconsin
Indiana Dunes National Lakeshore, Indiana
Pictured Rocks National Lakeshore, Michigan
Sleeping Bear Dunes National Lakeshore, Michigan

National Monuments

National monuments differ from national parks in that they can be created by either an act of Congress or a presidential proclamation, and can be managed by the National Park Service, Bureau of Land Management, the U.S. Forest Service, or the Fish and Wildlife Service. Several former national monuments have been "promoted" to national parks, such as Grand Teton and Grand Canyon. There are 177 national monuments in the U.S.

National Forests

There are nearly 200 million acres of public lands managed by the National Forest Service, These lands are designated for "multiple use," including recreational activities such as boating, fishing, and even skiing!

National Park Pass

The best way to visit the national parks is to buy a park pass, which is good for a year. Usually it takes only a few trips to the national parks, and it pays for itself. The pass isn't just good for national parks, either. Take a look at all the ways you can use your national park pass.

National parks
National monuments
National wildlife refuges
National forests
National grasslands
Lands managed by Bureau of Land Management
Lands managed by Bureau of Reclamation

All fourth graders can sign up for a free park pass through a special government program called *Every Kid in a Park*. Learn more about it at everykidinapark.gov.

Leave No Trace Principles for Kids Visiting the Parks

- Know Before You Go
- Choose The Right Path
- Trash Your Trash
- Leave What You Find
- Be Careful With Fire
- Respect Wildlife
- Be Kind To Other Visitors

Photo Credits

EASTERN PARKS

Acadia—Rocky Ocean Drive Coast, NPS/Kristi Rugg; Baker Island Skiff, NPS; Peregrine Chicks, NPS; Fall Carriage Road, NPS; Doe, NPS; Ranger with Kids, NPS; Kid with Microscope, NPS; Blueberries, Chris Dag; Maine Moose, Dana Moos

Cuyahoga Valley—Great Blue Heron, J. Todd Poling; Painted Turtle, Joanne; Steam Train, Joanne; Towpath, Joanne; Raccoon, Benny Mazur; Brandywine Falls, Tim Evanson

Shenandoah—Fall Color, NPS; Hikers on Old Rag, NPS; Whitetail Deer, NPS; Bobcat, NPS; Junior Ranger, NPS; Opossum, Andrew C.; Scarlet Tanager, A. Drauglis; Tulip Poplar, Rex Hammock

Great Smoky Mountains—Trail Sign, Ken Lund; Black Bear, Phil Horton; Little River Road, Jared; Grotto Falls with Kids, pfly; Elk, Mark Stoffan; Black Chinned Red Salamander, Todd Pierson; Cerulean Warbler, DiaGraphic

Hot Springs—Hot Springs, Ken Lund; Bath House Row, Rob Stoppable; Pine Oak Hickory, Ken Lund; Dramatic Pointing, U.S. Department of the Interior/Becky Hays; Red-bellied Woodpecker, Tanya Impeartrice; Green Treefrog, Brian Gratwicke; Raccoon, Tambako the Jaguar

Mammoth Cave—Cave Crayfish, NPS; Ruins of Karnak, NPS; Saltwater Leaching Vats, NPS; Bike Riding Trail, NPS; Green River, James St. John; Little Brown Bat, NPS; Mammoth Dig, Bo Gordy-Stith; Trout Lily, Nicholas A. Tonelli

Congaree—Boardwalk, Ken Lund; Green Anole, Richard; Loblolly Pine, Chris M. Morris; Canoe, Ryon Edwards; Spanish Moss, Hunter Desportes; Bald Cypress, NPS; Barred Owl, David Hill

Everglades—Alligator, NPS; Panther, NPS; Anhinga, NPS; Aerial Shot, NPS; Sawgrass, NPS; Sunset, NPS; Junior Rangers, NPS; Kids with Ranger, NPS; Manatee, NPS

Biscayne—American Crocodile, NPS; Underwater, NPS; Hawksbill Sea Turtle, Silke Baron; Manatees, psyberartist; Boca Chita Key, NPS; Totten Key Aerial, NPS; Mangrove, NPS

Dry Tortugas—Reef Fish, NPS/John Dengler; Seaplane, NPS/John Dengler; Brain Coral, NPS/John Dengler; Frigate Bird, Don Faulkner; Loggerhead Sea Turtle, Brian Gratwicke; Loggerhead Babies, U.S. Fish & Wildlife Service; Green Sea Turtle, Laszlo Ilyes

Virgin Islands—Trunk Bay, Rennett Stowe; Trunk Bay Trail Map, David Fulmer; Sugar Factory Ruins, David Fulmer; Sugar Mill, Navin Rajagopalan; Bulldog Bat, Mark Spangler; Sea Grass, Connie Ma; Small Coral Colony, National Oceanic and Atmospheric Administration; Kids Scuba Diving, VISIONS Service Adventures

MIDWEST PARKS

Isle Royale—Ferry, Joe Ross; Chippewa Harbor Sunset, Ray Dumas; Siskiwit River, Ray Dumas; Loons, Ray Dumas; Bull Moose, Ray Dumas; Wolf, USFWS Midwest; Wolf Track, Ray Dumas

Voyageurs—Scenic, JCK photos; River Otters, USFWS Midwest; Beavers, NWF; Paddling, USFWS Midwest; Boat Safety, USFWS Midwest; Kids, USFWS Midwest

Theodore Roosevelt—Badlands, NPS/Mark Meyers; Black-tailed Prairie Dog, NPS/Jeff Zyland; Black-footed Ferret, NPS; Bison, NPS/Jeff Zyland; Pronghorn, NPS/Laura Thomas; Maltese Cross Cabin, Mike Oswald; Prairie Rattlesnakes, Jared Tarbell; Western Meadowlark, NPS/Larry McAfee

Badlands—Bighorn Sheep, NPS/Lee McDowell; Bison, NPS/Lee McDowell; Kids, NPS; Kids Hiking, NPS/Dudley Edmondson; Bigfoot Overlook, NPS/Lee McDowell; Norbeck Pass, NPS/Shaina Niehans; Matthew with Fossil, NPS/Larry McAfee; Swift Fox, U.S. Fish & Wildlife Service (Mountain-Prairie)

Wind Cave—Boxwork, NPS; Wind Cave Prairie, David Fulmer; Storm over Wind Cave, Justin Meissen; Ponderosa Pine, Jay Sterner; Prairie Falcon, U.S. Fish & Wildlife Service (Mountain-Prairie); Prairie Falcon, U.S. Fish & Wildlife Service (Mountain-Prairie); White Penstemon, Jeff B

MOUNTAIN WEST PARKS

Glacier—U-Valley Going to the Sun Road, Ken Lund; Glacier National Park, Dave Sizer; Mountain Goats, Lee Coursey; Grizzly Bear, Pat Williams; Bus, Loco Steve; Bear Grass, NPS; Harlequin Duck, Peggy Cadigan; Golden-mantled Ground Squirrel, Andy Reago & Chrissy McClarren; Bighorn Sheep, Christian Grimm

Yellowstone—River Rafting, NPS; Mountain Goat with her Kid, NPS; Fresh Snow on Soda Butte Creek, NPS; Grey Wolf, NPS; Bison, NPS; Old Faithful, Jim Peaco; Grand Canyon of the Yellowstone, Jim Peaco; Grizzly Bear, Jim Peaco; Yellowstone Cutthroat Trout, Neal Herbert; Red Squirrel, Neal Herbert; Grand Prismatic Spring, Jim Peaco

Grand Teton—Scenic, Jeff Gunn; Willows, NPS; Bison, NPS; River Otter, U.S. Fish & Wildlife Service (Pacific Southwest); Masked Shrew, Chris and Tilde Stuart; Aspen, Jeff Gunn; Elk, Don DeBold; Trumpeter Swans, USFWS Midwest

Rocky Mountain—Trail Ridge Road, NPS; Hallet Peak and Dream Lake, NPS; Bighorn Rams on the Tundra, NPS; Beaver, NPS/Kent Miller; Young Elk in the Sun, Jacob W. Frank; American Dipper, Greg Schechter; Aspens from below, David Pinigis

Great Sand Dunes—Tiger Beetle, NPS; Pronghorns, NPS; Sandhill Cranes, NPS; Girl Sandboarding, NPS/Patrick Myers; Great Sand Dunes in Fall, NPS/Patrick Myers; Kids Floating Down Medano Creek, NPS/Patrick Myers

Black Canyon of the Gunnison—Inner Canyon, NPS/Lisa Lynch; Island Peaks, NPS/Lisa Lynch; Striped (Western Texas) Whipsnake, NPS/Cookie Ballou; Peregrine Falcon, Alan Wu; Mule Deer, Yellowstone National Park

Mesa Verde—Coyote, NPS; Mule Deer, NPS; Step House, NPS; Cliff Palace, NPS/Sandy Groves; Juniper Titmouse, Alan Schmierer; Mesa Verde, Kyle Magnuson; Porcupine, U.S. Fish & Wildlife Service (Midwest)

SOUTHWEST PARKS

Carlsbad Caverns—Natural Entrance, NPS/Peter Jones; Queen's Chamber, NPS/Peter Jones; Witch's Finger, NPS/Peter Jones; Cave Cricket, Beatrice Murch; Mormon Tea, Jimmy Thomas; Ringtails Eating, Tambako the Jaguar

Guadalupe Mountains—Salt Lake, NPS; Summer Wildflowers, NPS; Javelina, Alan Levine; Guadalupe Hermoa, Brandon Satterwhite; Phainopepla, Daniel Plumer; Alligator Juniper, Homer Edward Price; Family, Jonathan Cutrer; Greater Roadrunner, Peter Wilton

Big Bend—Canoeing Mariscal Canyon, NPS/Jennette Jurado; Family Hiking in Winter, NPS/Jennette Jurado; Casa Grande and Window View, NPS/Reine Wonite; Girl on Rio Grande, David; Big Bend Bluebonnet, Dr. Thomas G. Barnes; colima warbler, Ross Nussbaumer/NPL/Minden Pictures; Big Bend Slider Turtle, Steve Hillebrand

Saguaro—Cristate Saguaro, NPS; Grand-Daddy Saguaro, NPS; Lesser Long-nosed Bats, Alan Schmierer; Gila Woodpecker on Cactus, Mike's Birds; Coati, Tony Auston

Petrified Forest—Evening Primrose, NPS; Field Trip with Park Paleontologist, NPS; Jasper Forest, NPS; Mountain Lion Petroglyph, NPS; Blue Mesa Formation, NPS; Horned Lark, Greg Schechter; Black-tailed Jackrabbit, Kathy & Sam; Boy Measuring, NPS/Susan McElhinney; Coyote, Stars Apart

Grand Canyon—Mule Deer, NPS; Intense Rafting, NPS; California Condor, Brian Gatlin; Gentle Rafting, Mark Lellouch; Hiking Along Ledge, Michael Quinn; Desert View Watchtower, Mike Buchheit

UTAH AND NEVADA PARKS

Arches—Delicate Arch, Jeff Keacher; Western Scrub Jay, Alan Schmierer; Western Collared Lizard, NPS/Casey Hodnett; Mule Deer, NPS/Kait Thomas; Bighorn Sheep, NPS/Neal Herbert; Balanced Rock, NPS/Kait Thomas; Delicate Arch, Theresa Howell; Fiery Furnace, NPS/Chris Wonderly; Double O Arch, NPS/Kait Thomas

Canyonlands—Sunrise at the Needles, NPS/Neal Herbert; Schafer Trail, Robbie Shade; White-tailed Antelope Ground Squirrel, NPS/Brad Sutton; Pinyon Jay, Seabamirum; Bobcat, docentjoyce; Green River, NPS/Andrew Kuhn; Learning about the Park, Peter & Joyce Grace; Mesa Arch, NPS/Kirsten Kearse

Capitol Reef—Capitol Reef, NPS/Jacob Frank; Side-blotched Lizard, Mechanoid Dolly; Canyon Treefrog, NPS/Caitlin Ceci; Golden Eagle, Tony Hisgett; Panorama Point, NPS/Chris Roundtree; The Fruita District with Cabin, Robb Hannawacker; The Fruita District, NPS/Chris Roundtree

Bryce Canyon—Fairyland Loop, Nicolas Vollmer; Mountain Lion, Eric Kilby; Uinta Chipmunk, Jean-Claude Langevin; Utah Prairie Dog, U.S. Fish & Wildlife Service/Tom Koerner; Hoodoos, Moyan Brenn; Kid Drawing Hoodoos, daveynin; Willow Flycatcher, Alan Schmierer

Zion—Court of the Patriarchs, Adam Schallau ; Mexican Spotted Owl, NPS; Coyote, NPS/Sarah Sito; Peregrine Falcon, NPS; The Narrows, Christopher Michel; Sunrise, Don Graham

Great Basin—Wheeler Peak, Frank Kovalchek; American Badger, James Perdue; Common Raven, Don Graham; Pygmy Rabbit, R. Dixon and H. Ulmschneider; Bristlecone Pine, J. Brew; Lehman Caves, Frank Kovalcheck; Scenic, Frank Kovalcheck

CALIFORNIA PARKS

Joshua Tree—Scenic, NPS/Brad Sutton; Gambel's Quail, NPS; Western Chuckwalla, NPS; Cactus Wren, NPS; Desert Tortoise, NPS; Skull Rock, Tony Webster; Learning the history of the Park, NPS/Sarah Dumont; Sunset, NPS/Brad Sutton; Signs, Ken Lund

Channel Islands—Scenic, David Wan; California Sea Lions, Ken Lund; Island Fox, Andy Rusch; Island Scrub-jay, U.S. Fish & Wildlife Service/Kirk Wain; Anacapa Island Light Station, Aaron Zhong; Natural Bridge, Lisa Andres; Gray Whale, Isabella Acatauassu Alves

Pinnacles—Scenic, David Fulmer; Acorn Woodpecker, Andy Reago & Chrissy McClarren; California Red-legged Frog, U.S. Fish & Wildlife Service (Pacific Southwest); Black-tailed Deer, Ken Lund; Bear Gulch Cave, Ken Lund; California Condor, U.S. Fish & Wildlife Service (Pacific Southwest); Acmon Blue Butterfly, CountryMouse13

Death Valley—Dante's View, Gary Crabbe ; Mojave Desert Sidewinder, Minden; Greater Roadrunner, Dawn Beattie; Desert Tortoise, Philip Kahn; Zabriskie Point, Rick Mortensen; Scotty's Castle, Craig Mirkin; Bighorn Sheep, Cary Bass-Deschenes; The Race Track, G Dan Mitchell; Sea Level Sign, Ken Lund

Sequoia & Kings Canyon—Scenic, Alberto Carrasco-Casado; Bighorn Sheep, Don DeBold; Black Bear, NPS/Neal Herbert; California Kingsnake, U.S. Fish & Wildlife Service (Pacific Southwest); California Newt, Steve Jurvetson; Cabin, Vince Villamon; General Sherman, US Dept. of the Interior

Yosemite—Glacier Point, Bruce Tuten; Grizzly Giant, Steve Dacosta; Black Bear, U.S. Fish & Wildlife Service (Midwest); Sierra Garter Snake, Vlad Butsky; California Ground Squirrel, S. Rae; Yosemite Toad, U.S. Fish & Wildlife Service (Pacific Southwest); Steller's Jay, SD Dirk; El Capitan, Todd Petrie; Hiking, U.S. Fish & Wildlife Service (Pacific Southwest); Mist Trail, David Fulmer

Lassen Volcanic—Scenic, NPS; Golden-mantled Ground Squirrel, NPS; California Tortoiseshell Butterfly, NPS; White-headed Woodpecker, Alan Schmeirer; Pacific Treefrog, Marshal Hedin; Boiling Springs Lake, NPS; Terminal Geyer, NPS

Redwood—Foothill Trail, Redwood Coast; California Sea Lions, Alan Schmierer; Marbled Murrelet, US Dept. of Agriculture; Roosevelt Elk, Bureau of Land Management; Banana Slug, Tim Wilson; Hiking "through" the forest, Ilya Katsnelson; Driving "through" the forest, Amy Selleck

PACIFIC NORTHWEST PARKS

Crater Lake—Scenic, Jonathan Miske; Bald Eagle, Oregon Dept. of Fish & Wildlife; Northern Spotted Owl, Kameron Perensovich; Bull Trout, USA; Coastal Tailed Frog, MYN/JP Lawrence; Crater Lake Lodge, Andy Melton

Mount Rainier—Rainier Reflections, NPS; Rainier Wildflowers, NPS; Deer in Wildflowers, NPS; Black-tailed Deer, Lee Coursey; Douglas Squirrel, U.S. Fish & Wildlife Service/Peter Pearsall; Steller's Jay, SD Dirk; American Marten, U.S. Forest Service; Common Raven, Ingrid Taylar

North Cascades—Scenic, Rachel Samanyi; Long-toed Salamander, Oregon Department of Fish & Wildlife/Simon Wray; Black-tailed Deer, U.S. Fish & Wildlife Service/Peter Pearsall; Wolverine, Barney Moss; Pika, NPS/Jon LaVasseur; North Cascades Highway, Navin Rajagopalan

Olympic—Scenic, Jason Pratt; Olympic Yellow-Pine Chipmunk, Francesco Veronesi; Sea Otters, U.S. Fish & Wildlife Service; Olympic Marmot, Scott Cox; Sol Duc Falls, David Dulmer; Investigating the Park, Chris Booth

PACIFIC ISLAND PARKS

Hawai'i Volcanoes—View from Summit, Ron Cogswell; Rainbow, Ron Cogswell; Sign, Eli Duke; Lava Tube, Prayitno Hadinata; Lava Flow, Thomas Tunsch; Red Lehua, Anissa Wood; 'I'iwi Honeycreeper, U.S. Fish & Wildlife Service/Donald Metzner; Hawaiian Hawksbill Sea Turtle, U.S. Fish & Wildlife Service (Pacific); Hawaiian Silversword, David Eickhoff; Entrance to a Lava Tube, Robert Linsdell

Haleakala—Scenic, Navin Rajoagopalan; Happy Face Spider, Jeff Wright; Monk Seal, James Abbot; Hawaiian Hoary Bat, Forrest & Kim Starr; Haleakala Crater, NPS; Nene, NPS; Ahinahina, NPS/A. Rulison

America Samoa—Si'u Point Trail, U.S. Department of the Interior; Pola Island Trail, U.S. Department of the Interior; Pago Pago Harbor, NPS of America Samoa/Tavita Togia; Humpback Whales, texasus1; Hawksbill Sea Turtle, U.S. Fish & Wildlife Service (Pacific)/Caroline Rogers; White-collared Kingfisher, Raghunath T

ALASKA PARKS

Denali—Scenic, NPS/Tim Rains; Grey Wolf, NPS/Ken Conger; Moose, NPS/Kent Miller; Caribou, NPS/Lian Law; Dall Sheep, NPS/Lian Law; Grizzly Bear, NPS/Daniel A. Leifheit; Riding a Dogsled, NPS/Jacob W. Frank; Hiking the Park, NPS; Reflection in Lake, NPS/Tim Rains

Gates of the Arctic—Scenic, NPS/Penny Knuckles; Caribou, NPS/Zak Richter; Musk Ox, U.S. Fish & Wildlife Service; Arctic Foxes, Eric Kilby; Northern Lights, United States Air Force/Joshua Strang; Noatak River from Air, NPS

Kobuk Valley—Sand Dunes, NPS/Neal Herbert; Students Enjoying the Dunes, WesternArctic; Arctic Ground Squirrel, NPS/Alex Vanderstuyf; Kobuk Locoweed, WesternArctic; Caribou Swimming, WesternArctic; Air Taxi, NPS/Neal Herbert

Lake Clark—Scenic, Caitlin Marr; Lake and Flowers, NPS/Warren Hill; Canada Lynx, NPS/Jacob W. Frank; Wolverine, U.S. Fish & Wildlife Service (Mountain-Prairie); Bald Eagle, NPS; Dolly Varden, NPS; Sockeye Salmon, Bureau of Land Management

Katmai—Brooks Falls, Christoph Strässler; Valley of Ten Thousand Smokes, Christoph Strässler; Red Fox, NPS/Jacob W. Frank; Northern Fur Seals, Public Domain; White-crowned Sparrow, Sandy Brown Jensen; A Brown Bear Enjoying a Sockeye Salmon, Christoph Strässler

Kenai Fjords—Bear Glacier, NPS; Exit Glacier, US Dept. of the Interior; Steller Sea Lions, National Oceanic and Atmospheric Administration; Pacific White-sided Dolphins, NOAA National Marine Sanctuaries/Robert Schwemmer; Black Oystercatcher, U.S. Fish & Wildlife Service/Peter Pearsall; Horned Puffins, U.S. Fish & Wildlife Service

Wrangell-St. Elias—Scenic, NPS/Bryan Petrtyl; Mt. St. Elias, NPS/Bryan Petrtyl; Kennecott Mines, NPS/Matthew Yarbrough; Dall Sheep, NPS/Bryan Petrtyl; Trumpeter Swans, NPS/Bryan Petrtyl; Moose, NPS

Glacier Bay—Johns Hopkins Glacier, NPS; Johns Hopkins Inlet, NPS/C. Behnke; A Pair of Dall's Porpoises, Greg Schechter; Sea Otter, Gregory Smith; Steller Sea Lion, National Oceanic and Atmospheric Administration; Tufted Puffin, Nic McPhee; Orcas, Mike Charest